D0049597

The
NEXT CHRISTIANS

The
NEXT CHRISTIANS

The Good News About
the End of Christian America

Gabe Lyons

DOUBLEDAY

New York • London • Toronto • Sydney • Auckland

ꀎ
DOUBLEDAY

DOUBLEDAY and the DD colophon are registered trademarks of
Random House, Inc.

Published in association with Yates and Yates, www.yates2.com.

Library of Congress Cataloging-in-Publication Data

Lyons, Gabe, 1975–
The next Christians : the good news about the end of Christian America /
Gabe Lyons. — 1st ed.
p. cm.
Includes bibliographical references (p.   ).
1. Christianity—United States—21st century.   2. United States—Church
history—21st century.   I. Title.
BR526.L97 2010
277.3'083—dc22   2010006089

ISBN 978-0-385-52984-6

Printed in the United States of America

Design by Lauren Dong

1 3 5 7 9 10 8 6 4 2

First Edition

CONTENTS

PART I
THE WORLD IS CHANGING

ONE

A Fading Reality

SEVEN YEARS AGO, I WAS TWENTY-SEVEN YEARS OLD AND embarrassed to call myself *Christian*. This was especially odd because I was raised in a Christian home, graduated from a Christian college, and then served as vice president of a prominent Christian organization. By all accounts, I should have been one of Christianity's biggest fans.

Unfortunately, I began to notice that the perceptions my friends and neighbors had about Christians were incredibly negative. In fact, their past experiences with anything labeled *Christian* had sent them running in the opposite direction. Ironically, I came to empathize with their views. Having grown up in a Christian bubble myself, I witnessed countless instances when the lives of Christ followers were incongruent with Jesus's call to be loving, engaged, sacrificial, unselfish, and compassionate contributors to culture. The angst these experiences created would scare anyone from taking a second look at Jesus.

I was deeply burdened by this trend and about the loss of Christian influence in our culture. So, with just a few months of savings in the bank and our second child on the way, my wife, Rebekah, and I decided I should quit my job and pursue a new vocation. We resolved to launch a nonprofit organization and make our first project the commissioning of research that would help us understand the perceptions that sixteen- to twenty-nine-year-olds have about Christians.

The study confirmed many of our fears about the negative perceptions I had experienced. An overwhelming percentage of non-Christians sampled said they perceived Christians as judgmental, hypocritical, too political, and antihomosexual, among other things.

In the truest sense, the research revealed what happens when Christians act *unchristian*. The study was released in a book by the same name. It soon became a bestseller, confirming that our findings resonated with the general public.

But it also exposed something bigger that has been going on. The Christian faith is quickly losing traction in Western culture, not only as a result of unchristian behavior, as significant as that is, but because we haven't recognized our new reality and adapted.

In years since, our nonprofit has convened rising Christian leaders at various locations across America to have conversations about what they see occurring in the Christian movement and how they are uniquely living out their faith. We began to ask important questions about the role Christians should play in society:

What does mission look like in America in the twenty-first century?
How should the message of the Gospel go forward?
What does it mean to be a Christian in a world that is
 disenchanted with our movement?

Every generation must ask these questions as they seek to confront the unique challenges of their own eras. In modern times, thinkers like Reinhold Niebuhr, C. S. Lewis, Francis Schaeffer, Os Guinness, and Lesslie Newbigin have reflected on the relationship between Christians and culture in the twentieth century. Even now, a diverse group of future-thinking leaders are offering insight into how the next generation might navigate our current cultural waters.

Research shows that over 76 percent of Americans self-identify as Christian.[1] Yet I wonder how many of us are proud to carry that label. Are we hiding our faith in our back pockets? My guess is that many feel much like I did at twenty-seven when they encounter non-Christians at work, in coffee shops, on campus, in their neighborhoods, at weekend parties, or working out at the gym. You may be dumbfounded that there are 76 percent of "us" and yet little unity in what we collectively represent.

After observing cultural trends, collecting data, and having hundreds of conversations with Christian leaders, I see a new way forward. There is a whole movement of Christians—evangelicals, mainline Protestants, Orthodox, Pentecostals, and others—asking these same questions and offering meaningful answers. They want to be a force for restoration in a broken world even as we proclaim the Christian Gospel. They want the label *Christian* to mean something good, intelligent, authentic, true, and beautiful.

* * *

DURING A GATHERING convened by our nonprofit, we were offered a rare invitation to visit the home of Billy Graham in nearby Montreat, North Carolina. Typically, it's best to keep an experience like that to yourself, where its magnitude will never tarnish, but I feel compelled to share it with you here because of the significance of what took place.

The slow ascent up the winding mountain driveway in Montreat mirrored my rising anticipation. Going to meet with this great evangelist in his storied log cabin home nestled in the Blue Ridge Mountains didn't feel real—I was rapt with expectation.

The leaves were changing color and produced a kaleidoscope of hues—from green to brown, yellow, orange, and red—on the surrounding mountain faces. After passing through the entry gate protecting his mountaintop home, we were greeted by an older woman, a caretaker of sorts. That day, she had taken it upon herself to care for us as well. Her kind but weathered hands served up one of my favorites—chocolate chip cookies and an old-fashioned bottle of Coke. It felt surprisingly warm and hospitable, like a weekend trip to Grandma's house.

While waiting to be led back to Mr. Graham's study on this crisp autumn day in September, we sat in old rocking chairs on the back porch. (I later learned these chairs had been gifts from President Lyndon Johnson from his ranch in Texas.)

Taking in the picturesque view, I could understand why Montreat had been the place this man chose to call home for more than fifty years. The quiet, pastoral scene was splendid. With no other man-made structure in sight, it was an ideal place of respite for the family of a world figure. The simplicity of his log cabin, meadowlike backyard, well-worn antique furniture, and pictures of family and friends playing together gave me a glimpse into this beloved saint's humanity.

I couldn't help considering the countless accolades assigned to his life. He had audience with the world's most powerful leaders, providing spiritual counsel to seven U.S. presidents. His generous tone and compelling life have marked everyone

who's known him. He shaped our world very personally by leading tens of millions of everyday people to Christ. Having trav-
eled the world many times over, the eighty-nine-year-old
evangelist had witnessed what God was up to in the world. It
was a once in a lifetime opportunity to converse with one of the
most sought-after, respected, and revered leaders of the twentieth century. Our time together didn't disappoint.

As we walked back to his study, his companions—five dogs
that kept him company day and night—greeted us. Though his
body was undeniably old, his mind was sharp. Hearing had become a chore for him, so we raised our voices to introduce ourselves. I sat down in front of Mr. Graham in a chair whose
previous occupants included world leaders, famous entertain-
ers, and—just two weeks prior—a presidential candidate hoping to gain his support.

I came prepared to learn. I had no intention of saying much,
planning instead to glean his wisdom. For what must have been
thirty minutes or so, I quietly listened until I finally gained the
courage to speak.

I carefully explained our work to educate and expose church
and cultural leaders to the changes in our world, and more important, what opportunities lay ahead. Mr. Graham seemed
genuinely curious to hear about what we do. I continued by telling him about some of the leaders our organization convened
regularly, innovators within every sphere of society. From the
arts to medicine and education, I explained that they were
young and the best at what they did. I described how these leaders were leveraging their talent for the benefit of others—
creating microfinance banks that were lending hundreds of
millions of dollars to the poor, building wells throughout the
third world, developing media campaigns to increase awareness

about adoption—and were serious about restoring culture. I had a hunch that these remarkably likeminded individuals were the next wave of Christians in the world, but I wanted to know if he agreed.

He reflected on everything I had been sharing with him before a smile walked the sides of his face. "Back when we did these big crusades in football stadiums and arenas, the Holy Spirit was really moving—and people were coming to Christ as we preached the Word of God," the evangelist said. "But today, I sense something different is happening. I see evidence that the Holy Spirit is working in a new way. He's moving through people where they work and through one-on-one relationships to accomplish great things. They are demonstrating God's love to those around them, not just with words, but in deed."

As he spoke, something began to crystallize inside me. It was as if all the observations I'd collected over a decade were being summed up in the sage words of this iconic figure. He had seen the best of what twentieth-century Christianity had to offer, yet was in tune with something new.

I left Montreat with a quiet confidence that day—not only because I had been in the presence of a great and godly man, but also because he had confirmed in succinct terms the things I'd been observing. Reflecting on his words challenged me to continue cultivating this mind-set throughout the body of believers across our developing landscape.

*   *   *

NOT LONG AFTER my conversation with Graham, Rebekah and I celebrated our tenth wedding anniversary with a trip to Europe. Since it was the off season, we were braced for the wet, dreary weather typical of London and Paris at that time of year.

However, to our amazement, the region experienced a run of the warmest days on their calendar in a century. Instead of being wet, bundled up, and longing for the warmth of the cozy Hôtel du Louvre, we enjoyed long walks in the cool breeze—wearing sweaters and scarves, leaving the coats behind. It was enchanting. The architecture, museums, and cafés were brimming with energy. Experiencing millennium-old culture that was still full of life refreshed my soul.

One portion of our travels that I was particularly excited about was our rail trip from London to Paris on the famed EuroStar. I had read about its top speeds of 190 miles per hour as it glides under the English Channel and through the French countryside en route to Paris's Gare du Nord. When we boarded the train, I knew we were in for a great experience.

As I leaned back in my seat, the headrest curved perfectly around my neck—like an apparatus designed for intense flight, somehow befitting such a modernized tour of these storied countries. The ride across Britain was routine and somewhat metropolitan. Then as the train entered the Channel Tunnel, it picked up speed. The blur of lights gave the impression of flying through space. By the time we emerged in France, I felt transported. Leaning back in my seat, I stared out at the countryside as it sped past me like an abbreviated survey of French history. I'd flown *over* this landscape at high speed before, but never *through* it.

The foreground was an imperceptible blur of vegetation broken only by the occasional buildings and bridges. My eyes were drawn to the horizon as a steady succession of towns and villages rose into view along the way. We passed through Calais, then Lille, as we made our way toward Paris.

A pattern seemed to be emerging. In each community I saw

a town center surrounded by trees and an occasional cottage. And at the heart of every town I could see a church steeple appear among the treetops and above the storefronts. It was consistent with what I knew of ancient urban architecture, that the steeple was designed to be the tallest structure in a city, representing the sacred belief that the church should be the closest point between heaven and earth, God and humanity.

Miles apart, those communities now seemed lined up almost side by side, as if to make a collective statement for my observation: *The church used to occupy the center of culture in the West.* For a brief moment, I reminisced about what once was. Not too long ago, children would frequent their church for much-needed education and moral training. In this prime location, new families were welcomed to town and volunteer needs were addressed before singing and prayer meetings would resume. Houses of worship were also places of great artistic and musical innovation. Many of history's greatest creative minds birthed their monolithic works within these hallowed confines.

Indeed, where the church in Europe once held a place of significant influence, by the end of the twentieth century it was almost completely irrelevant.[2] Even the design of their communities bore evidence to it. The steeples that once stood for spiritual enlightenment have been reduced to minor tourist attractions. They better serve the needs of visiting amateur photographers than the lost souls of the people in their own communities.

Some culture watchers say that when we survey the contours of Europe's religious landscape, we are staring America's future in the face. While there is no way to verify these predictions, from my experience and all the evidence I've collected surrounding the church and citizens of our country, America isn't far behind.

What began as a creeping intuition that led me to launch a new organization had become a nagging reality that significant changes were under way. My trip to Europe and Montreat seemed to represent the two ends of our current situation. In Montreat, I met with an icon from Christianity's past who recognizes how the faith is presently shifting. In Europe, I seemingly caught a glimpse of America's more secular future. Positioned between these poles was the empirical research we had commissioned and the hundreds of conversations with a new generation of Christian leaders. Each situation echoed the sentiment that many Christians have lost confidence in their faith. Our movement, as a whole, was quickly declining in the West.

I believe this moment is unlike any other time in history. Its uniqueness demands an original response. If we fail to offer a different way forward, we risk losing entire generations to apathy and cynicism. Our friends will continue to drift away, meeting their need for spiritual transcendence through other forms of worship and communities of faith that may be less true but more authentic and appealing.

Maybe you know someone like my friend Dan. He grew up around the church and considers himself a Christian. At the age of thirty-four, he finds himself at the center of huge international business deals. Dan's a rainmaker type, and when his complex transactions are successful, they can raise the GDP of entire nations! But as we were catching up on our lives one day, he dropped a bomb on me. He said, "I hope this won't shock you, but I don't call myself a Christian anymore. I follow Christ as faithfully as I can, but I don't ever want to be associated with what that word, or that 'brand,' has come to represent in the world."

I asked him what he felt the consequences would be for him professionally or socially if people were to know about his faith. He responded with a cynical prediction, "It would be the death of my business career to be marked as a Christian because of all the baggage it represents." Our current dilemma is that there are thousands of people just like Dan out there, and you may be one of them. Maybe you haven't left the faith altogether, but you find yourself increasingly uncomfortable with what it has become.

Do not be discouraged. God is at work at this very moment. He doesn't look upon our current cultural milieu and wring his hands as if he didn't see it coming. In the midst of unprecedented change, his people are rooting themselves in the fertile ground of our current age and celebrating what the Christian movement is becoming. As we confront the possibilities that tomorrow may hold, I invite you to not only study the facts. I urge you to reenvision your faith.

To enhance your experience while reading this book, go to www.nextchristians.com/enhanced to meet the author, see video content, and hear interviews with those this book describes.

TWO

The New Normal

I FIRST REALIZED THAT "CHRISTIAN AMERICA" WAS DEAD ON a cool morning in the middle of May. I had just arrived at "The Tannery"—the 140-year-old loft space where our team worked. Beside me, century-old long-leaf pine beams steady the bowed roof above while the maple hardwoods below bear the scars of turn-of-the-century saddle making.

I love that old, restored space. The smells of aged wood, permanently clouded windows, and countless stories held by its rugged brick walls captivate me.

I no sooner sat down at my desk than a colleague burst into my office. "Did you hear the news?" he shouted.

"What news? Tell me!" I said anxiously, while my index finger stumbled to tap refresh on my online news feed. As the words came out of his mouth, the headline loaded: FALWELL DEAD.

For over forty years, Jerry Falwell had been one of the most polarizing figures of American Christianity. And while his death made headlines in the national news, it was nothing short of a historical landmark for someone in my line of work. My first book, *UnChristian*, was in many ways to serve as a report card for influential Christians in modern culture. And Falwell had been chief among them.

Like many Christians, our team had ridden a roller coaster of mixed emotions in the wake of his exploits over the years. Some days, we celebrated his presence as a guardian of moral conviction. Others, we cringed at his bombastic statements that baited controversy and alienated the very cause he sought to promote.

In his heyday, Falwell was considered a force to be reckoned with on the American political scene. His organization, the Moral Majority, had ignited what some pundits refer to as "the evangelical voting block." His years of motivating the grass roots to vote their moral conscience on issues like abortion and same-sex marriage had driven millions to the polls. At its height, the Moral Majority claimed over 6 million registered members.[1] Some have even credited Falwell with paving the way for President Ronald Reagan's success in his first bid for the White House.

On May 15, 2007, his life was over. In one unexpected moment—at the age of seventy-three—he had been permanently retired from the movement he created. Jerry Falwell had come face-to-face with the one whose business he believed he was doing.

As I tuned into cable news later that day, stories about his life were consuming the airwaves. I was curious to see how the media would treat the subject. Would they platform respectful eulogies (a reasonable response to the death of a major public figure) or allow for an all-out assault on a controversial figure known for initiating the Religious Right movement in the United States?

I wouldn't have to wait long to find out. After a commercial break, CNN anchor Anderson Cooper asked the outspoken atheist Christopher Hitchens for his reaction:

COOPER: I'm not sure you believe in heaven, but, if you do, do you think Jerry Falwell is in it?

HITCHENS: No, and I think it's a pity that there isn't a hell for him to go to.

COOPER: What is it about him that brings up such vitriol?

HITCHENS: The empty life of this ugly little charlatan proves only one thing, that you can get away with the most extraordinary offenses to morality and to truth in this country if you will just get yourself called reverend. . . .

COOPER: Whether you agree or not with his reading of the Bible, you don't think he was sincere in what he spoke?

HITCHENS: No. I think he was a conscious charlatan and bully and fraud. And I think, if he read the Bible at all—and I would doubt that he could actually read any long book of— at all—that he did so only in the most hucksterish, as we say, Bible-pounding way.[2]

It was typical Hitchens. A classless performance, but his point was well made. Though the interview had ended, an unspoken sentiment that things had just begun lingered around our office. Falwell's death seemed a capstone for the slow, incremental shift we'd been following for more than a decade. For generations, many perceived our nation as "Christian America." Religiously, morally, politically, educationally—in virtually every way it could be measured—people had grown accustomed to the effects of the Christian movement.

Until June 25, 1962, nearly 40 million public school students were participating in daily, public prayers to the Christian God. Around the same time, authorities began forcibly removing copies of the Ten Commandments from courthouses, schoolhouses, and public spaces by the fistfuls. Christian icons, which once dominated American life, were fading away. Secularists and non-Christian religious voices began elbowing their way onto public stages and calling for recognition. Americans granted them entrée.

According to every data point we'd been studying, the landscape was changing. Christian America was fading into the background, and despite the culture war waged to counteract it, the shift was irreversible. To me, the death of Falwell seemed emblematic of the passing era. The Religious Right was giving way, while a pluralistic society—where all faiths would have a seat at the table—was settling in.

The Christian narrative has been almost completely replaced by a new story, and it has not gone unnoticed. "While we remain a nation decisively shaped by religious faith," writes Jon Meacham of *Newsweek*, "our politics and our culture are, in the main, less influenced by movements, and arguments of an explicitly Christian character than they were even five years ago."[3]

Hitchens had benefited personally from this shift. His *New York Times* bestseller *God Is Not Great: How Religion Poisons Everything* was a smashing success.

Consider CNN's choice to bring Hitchens on to air his grievances. They knew how outlandish and hateful he would be, but his view was given a legitimate place in the conversation—a clear sign that times had changed. Just a decade ago, no major network would have given a platform to an angry atheist like Hitchens.

CNN doubtlessly counted on Hitchens to provide their audience with shock and entertainment as they competed for ratings. He did not disappoint. But the showcasing of his views represented something much deeper, something more serious than just entertainment on a Tuesday afternoon. Judeo-Christian values no longer held sway in the public square.

The world of our grandparents was now barely visible in the cultural rearview mirror.

In this novel world, new rules were in place.

Now everything was in play.

May the best faith (or no faith at all) win.

* * *

A CLOUD OF frustration hung over my good friend Jeremy's head as he entered Sarabeth's, my favorite Upper East Side brunch spot in New York City. Normally a pretty even-keeled and intellectually balanced guy, he was visibly perplexed. After we exchanged the bare minimum of pleasantries, he revealed to me the source of his angst: *Zeitgeist*. It was the second time in a week that I had heard about this film—but now it had my attention. Jeremy, a longtime Manhattanite who had seen it all, was not normally hyped-up about conspiracy theories. But *Zeitgeist,* the latest online movie phenomenon, had his brain spinning. He looked disturbed.

Zeitgeist is a series of guerrilla films made to deconstruct societal institutions and cast doubt on deeply held cultural norms. It depicts most religions—and especially Christianity—as primarily systems of social control. The film claims, "Jesus was the Solar Deity of the Gnostic Christian sect, and like all other Pagan gods, he was a mythical figure." It suggests, "it was the political establishment that sought to historicize the Jesus figure for social control," and, "Christianity, along with all other theistic belief systems, is the fraud of the age."[4]

Its grungy attempt to enrage does not stop with Christianity. The film goes on to indict the U.S. government and, specifically, the Federal Reserve Bank. The film's producers boldly lay out a 9/11 conspiracy theory that charges the government with intentionally orchestrating the attacks on the Pentagon and World Trade Center. They claim the perceived terrorism was really all part of a bigger scheme to rescind civil liberties and create a false enemy that would bolster nationalism. *Zeitgeist* states, "criminal elements within the US government staged a 'false flag' terror attack on its own citizens, in order to manipulate public perception into supporting its agenda." According to the filmmakers, the government has supposedly been plotting this for years.[5]

That morning, Jeremy described to me two separate exchanges he had with friends during the previous week in which this film was the hot topic. His pals were convinced there was *something* to the film's message. They seemed persuaded that trusting in long-held societal beliefs was only for the naive; the intellectually honest rely on more than just tradition and authority—they find out for themselves.

Jeremy wasn't all that sure they were wrong.

He was shaken. Caught in the middle of two perspectives, he empathized with the skepticism his friends were voicing, because he, too, doubted what was really true anymore. He knew what he had been taught to believe, but he felt at a disadvantage in the face of such doubts. Beyond that, he wondered how his faith and allegiance to Jesus would ever make sense to such a skeptical audience. If he just told people what he believed, he'd be ignored or—worse yet—scoffed at.

His friends didn't want a defense of Christianity. They wanted something that could make sense out of their sordid lives—they wanted meaning, purpose—anything but the dusty claims of a two-thousand-year-old religion.

THE END OF THE WORLD AS WE KNOW IT

A perfect storm of change is brewing over America.

It's impossible for me to overstate this reality. Christianity has experienced many makeovers in the past two thousand years. The headliners include the First Council of Nicaea, the Christianization of Rome, the Crusades, and the Protestant Reformation, to name a few. Additionally, several eras have been dubbed a "Great Awakening." In each case, many sociological transitions triggered a defining moment in the life of the Christian faith. No culture shift is an island unto itself, but rather it is intimately connected to the historical moment from which it arises. So it is with the demise of Christian America.

Since the early 1900s, values like speed and progress have crept into prevailing thought—including faith. The industrial age struck like lightning and resulted in an emphasis on measurable parameters like conversions, attendance, and memberships at the inevitable expense of deeper experiences. In many towns, community gave way to corporate ladder climbing. Suddenly, people had less time to spend with neighbors and civic partners.

Without warning, the technological revolution shook hands with the industrial age and the resulting peak in accessibility to information pushed us into unknown territory. For centuries, there had been a steady increase in the dissemination of knowledge around the world, but this was different. The Internet and affordable computers gave birth to whole hosts of strange offspring such as PDAs, instant messaging, and open-source networks like Wikipedia. For the first time in history, the challenge of collecting data had been replaced by the need to understand the data we already possessed at our fingertips—right on our iPhones.

The implication is that anyone can claim "expert" status. In a matter of minutes, any preteen can set up a website or blog and gain a global hearing. More technology leads to more distractions from faith practices and more "expert" voices leads to more institutional skepticism.

The veils of mystery were lifted. Science was replacing blind faith, and the notion of accepting unexplainable phenomena or beliefs—once accepted via tradition—suddenly seemed implausible. Today, people no longer buy into moral ideas just because the cultural institutions say so. As a result, they're unloading conventional ideals and values by the truckload. Anything that can be verified firsthand is in. Everything else is out.

In the last twenty years, however, we've witnessed a phenomenon that is launching Christians into an unforeseen moment. Globalization and the emergence of a worldwide theater have torn down geographical boundaries. In the past, if you needed religious freedom, you could sail to a new world and pursue it. If the broader culture threatened your way of life, you could withdraw into a subculture to preserve it. But in our globalized landscape, these worlds increasingly overlap. There's no longer a geographical place where Christians can isolate, incubate, or regroup. Whatever they become, it will have to be within the broader context of life in America and the world.

The industrial age, the technological revolution, and globalization have converged to create a world where there are more distractions and less community, more religious skepticism and less institutional trust. These far-reaching cultural factors are peaking simultaneously. From the ideological and technological to the spiritual and physical, a new landscape is being fashioned before our very eyes. The shifts we are experiencing represent more than just a new political environment or the mere passing of generations.

Like many of our Christian ancestors, we find ourselves in a moment when the faith is changing drastically. The tectonic plates of our culture have moved and are now resettling. What's different about the current culture shift is the noticeable ways we're seeing this change manifest itself. This whirlwind of historical events has birthed three unprecedented cultural characteristics. Constantine never dreamed about anything like this.

Pluralistic

Pluralism rather than Christianity now marks America's public square.[6] Our nation is rediscovering and redefining religious liberty. Christianity's firm grip as the arbiter of morality in our nation has given way to an open playing field for the spiritually curious. Muslims roll out their prayer mats at airports. Buddhists build their temples in the suburbs. America has become "the world's most religiously diverse nation" and while Christians still make up a majority in America, Christian influentials are fading into the background.[7] Proponents of atheism command bestseller status while many Christians still proselytize on sidewalks.

In Jackson, Mississippi, a lesbian student donned a tuxedo for her senior picture. Not only did she feel empowered to deviate from cultural and moral norms, but when the school resisted, she simply pointed them to new precedents set in

Maryland, Florida, and Indiana that supported her desire. Rather than accept the inertia of tradition, the next generation doesn't hesitate to question it. When young adults are asked about allowing books by gay authors in local libraries or allowing an antireligious voice to give a public speech, about four in five say these activities are "permissible."[8]

Many Christians, especially those in the older generations, are visibly disconcerted, but the rest of the culture is noticeably content and comfortable with the new arrangement.[9] The media lauds congressional victories by practicing Muslims, and city mayors are often readily available for ribbon-cutting ceremonies at non-Christian houses of worship. On July 12, 2007, a Hindu chaplain led prayer in the U.S. Senate for the first time in history while everyday Americans went about business as usual.[10]

Regardless of how one characterizes the founding of this nation, few will argue that our country as we know it today can still be labeled "Christian America." Our nation's founders were *influenced* by Christian ideas, but they were also wise enough to structure America to allow for a pluralistic setting—a place where all faiths could be practiced and no faith would be given the upper hand.[11]

Now we've come full circle. The culture, it seems, has reached its threshold for this short-sheeted religion. More and more, God seekers are abandoning traditional Christian institutions in search of something else.

Not convinced? Research organizations like the Pew Forum on Religion and Public Life, LifeWay Research, *Time* magazine, and UCLA now say that most Protestant teens are leaving the faith after high school. Why? Fifty-one percent said they left their childhood religion because their spiritual needs were not being met.[12] Today, there are 31 percent fewer young people who are regular churchgoers than in the heat of the cultural revolution of the 1970s.[13]

Postmodern

The premise of the *Zeitgeist* film may sound ludicrous and outrageous to most of us. Yet films like *Zeitgeist* captivate young minds and fuel skepticism about certainty and belief. Over 50 million viewers have gone online to watch the film—the equivalent to one in every six Americans.

This should not surprise the culturally engaged. Twentysomethings have been primed for a film like *Zeitgeist*. Much of our world's messaging impels us to trust nothing and believe no one, especially people or institutions that claim absolute certainty. Why should they? Considering the maelstrom of fraudulence—corporate outrages by the likes of Enron and BP, misinformation about weapons of mass destruction, and highly publicized priest sex scandals—it's easy to see why suspicion runs rampant.

In this time of uncertainty, postmodern thinking has thrived. Stanley Grenz defined postmodernism as "a questioning, and even rejection, of the Enlightenment project and the foundational assumptions upon which it was built, namely, that knowledge is certain, objective and inherently good. Consequently it marks the end of a single worldview. Postmodernism resists unified, all-encompassing and universally valid explanations."[14] This skeptical attitude goes much deeper than a few major news stories over the last decade. Our cultural values in America (and throughout the West) have radically changed. At the street level, we've substituted modern, industrialized thinking with postmodern sensibilities.[15] The blinders are off and post-modernism is having significant consequences for the Christian movement. How could it not? If postmodernism rejects absolute certainty, it necessarily conflicts with a faith that claims to be certain about so much. Proclaiming in no uncertain terms to have the single answer to life's greatest problems, the Christian advance is being met with cynicism.

How are people reacting to the control Christianity has wielded over the thoughts and minds of society for so long? They are running as far away from it as possible. Rejecting the certainty and unproven assertions that modernism had promised, they brazenly challenge convention.

Post-Christian

In Europe, the church-centric towns Rebekah and I glided through perfectly symbolized the dominant role the church had played for centuries. But today, in Western Europe, Australia, New Zealand, Canada, and even the United States, the church has physically and conceptually lost its place in the center of public life. As Alan Hirsch and Michael Frost write, "By the end of the era of modernity in the mid-twentieth century, the Christian faith was no longer the center of Western culture."[16]

If you want to catch a glimpse of what a post-Christian setting looks like, head out to the suburbs. Life itself has changed, as most people no longer order their world around a geographic center. Suburban sprawl represents over 90 percent of residential growth in the past decade.[17] More important, the sociological structure of life has followed suit. Our daily patterns are structured around an eclectic mix of lifestyle choices.

Life is no longer localized to a neighborhood. Now life happens in many places. A person may choose one neighborhood for his residence and commute to a completely different part of town for his work. That same person may choose a gym on one side of town but prefer a coffee shop on the other. Family activities, meanwhile, introduce entirely new layers of places to show up on weeknights and weekends. In the process, the church—being the least of these demands—becomes relegated to the margins of life and activity.

In an effort to keep up, many suburban churches have followed closely behind—forced to choose locations in response to urban sprawl rather than function as a centerpiece of a holistic design. Some churches are now comfortably couched in streetside strip malls alongside dry cleaners and nail salons. This geographical relocation is perhaps a metaphor for the church's reduced role in people's lives. Instead of anchoring their center, some churches have become a convenient location where Christians can drop in without interrupting their normal routines.

Along the way, church leaders have been demoted in the public consciousness as well. Once relied upon as key allies for discussions about city issues and public life, they have lost their place at the table. They rub shoulders with the civic leaders in their communities with less frequency. And, unfortunately, many seem disinterested in investing in this relationship. Many churches are increasingly exhibiting less and less real influence in the communities where they're located. If they were gone tomorrow, one can't help wondering if anyone would notice.[18]

Likewise, urban churches struggle to pick up the pieces. As couples start families and then move out from their city centers, the church is thrust into transition. The combination of six-figure mortgages and empty pews is hardly a sustainable model for the churches abandoned by suburbanites. In many cases, once proud churches are left with a small but devoted elderly population that's been left behind. Fixed incomes and low volunteerism are telltale signs of a church on the decline.

The church has stealthily moved from the center of life to the periphery.[19] In the middle of it, we are not always aware that something significant is even happening. The developments driving it are slow and gradual, but the results are lasting. As humans, our tendency is to adapt, make good with the new challenges coming our way, and recalibrate to the new normal. In the last twenty years, these changes have slipped past many Christians who now feel a bit like a Christian frog inside a slow-boiling cultural kettle.

Rather than adapt, a significant group of Christians chose to react. They are resisting the change—unaware of the full implications of their response. Perhaps they long for the good ole days when life and faith seemed simpler—when things were black-and-white, clear, and logical—when Christian values were accepted at face value, no matter what else was going on in the world. As such, they have anchored themselves to the view that America is and should stay "a sacred Christian Nation." They think that God—as expressed in the Christian faith—was and should remain at the center of our public square. This faction focuses its energy on resistance despite the obvious trends rising all around it.

The culture war for Christian American values was the last stand for subcultural Christianity. By all accounts, that war is officially over. Even the most prominent Christian culture warriors cannot deny it. "The most basic contours of American culture have been altered," remarks Albert Mohler, president of the Southern Baptist Theological Seminary. "Clearly, there is a new narrative, a post-Christian narrative, that is animating large portions of this society."

The effort to see America formally defined and characterized according to Judeo-Christian ideals has been lost. Although a few skirmishes persist on the periphery, the momentum toward a new school of predominant thought is undeniable and irreversible.

*　*　*

A FEW YEARS ago, *Newsweek* published a double issue with the cover story titled "Spirituality in America."[20] It was an impressive dose of irony. For the last decade or so, respected religious leaders had been lamenting the death of Christian values in America. And now, the mainstream media were heralding Americans' quest for God.

Who was right?

It seems they both were. With convincing research, the *Newsweek* cover story pointed out that nearly 80 percent of Americans under the age of sixty described themselves as "spiritual." Almost two-thirds of them prayed every day and 75 percent acknowledged that a very important reason for their faith was to "forge a personal relationship with God."[21] But, at the same time, just over a third of Americans attended church weekly.[22]

The point was clear. Americans are spiritual, but they have begun to seek spiritual experiences outside the framework of traditional religions.[23]

When you stop and evaluate it, is this perfect storm of change all that bad? What if it's not a category 5 typhoon of spiritual death? What if it's not the bleak trumpet of apocalypse? What if it's actually a harnessable wind that can refill the sails of our faith?

I'm sure many Christians were disheartened by *Newsweek*'s findings. But they actually affirmed something I had been observing for some time: Most people *are* seeking truth. Americans may not be convinced that there is only one way to God, and they may be more skeptical toward Christianity than any other organized religion, but today they are compelled to experiment. They are open to new paths of spirituality; they are seeking approaches to faith that connect with the inner longings of their soul.

In fact, to a growing group of believers, this change represents another chapter in the story God is telling through a new generation. It's a welcome change from the out-of-control manipulations they've experienced when religion gets intertwined *too* closely with public life. They see it as an opportunity to send the Gospel out in fresh and compelling ways.

Could the end of Christian America become the stirrings of something beautiful? Is it possible to call a ceasefire in the culture war and still win the world? The generation of Christians you'll soon meet sees enormous opportunity *despite* all the shifts happening in society today.

They're optimistic.

They've had coffee shop conversations with friends and caught up on life in the cul-de-sac with neighbors. These Christians sense the deep hunger for meaning and purpose in the lives of their friends. They recognize these longings aren't really all that new. They are actually quite old and completely human. In the midst of change, the promise of good news is palpable. For those attuned to it, enormous possibilities await.

THREE

A Parody of Ourselves

A PRODUCER FOR LIONSGATE FILMS INVITED ME OUT TO LOS Angeles to weigh in on their strategy to reach Christians. Haley needed a cultural observer who understood the inner workings of the American Christian movement.

Three years earlier Mel Gibson's blockbuster *The Passion of the Christ* had rewritten the formula for marketing films to Christians. The faith community was now the crowned jewel of moviegoers. Whoever got to *them* next would be writing their ticket for the next decade. Haley's assignment was to accurately define the faithful for her marketing team. That's where I came in.

Haley asked me to help her make sense of the twenty-first-century Christian. As I had been recently discovering for myself, this would be a most difficult task. Sitting in their conference room in Santa Monica, I participated in one of the most interesting and challenging conversations I have ever had with a non-Christian.

Haley had worked on several major films as a producer and managed a large internal team for Lionsgate. She was not a Christian, but was motivated to understand the dynamics of the Christian community. If she could produce profits for her company, by opening a new channel of distribution, it all but ensured her a promotion.

Of course, Haley was looking for a simple demographic description of a people group. The clearer I could be, the better products they could develop and deliver to market. Easy enough, right?

What she hadn't anticipated and I frankly hadn't either was how difficult the explanation would be. She wanted a consumer market but I could give her only evidence of a fractured, confused community.

Using simple generalizations, I painted a picture of the different types of Christians that I've observed today. Responding to the changing world birthed by the twentieth century, American Christians now come in all shapes and sizes. From the do-gooders and casually spiritual to the Bible-thumpers and culture warriors, they cover every spectrum of the rainbow.

Making a film that could appeal to this broad array of Christians wouldn't be so simple.

As the in-depth research in *UnChristian* reveals, young people outside the faith perceived Christians as antihomosexual, judgmental, hypocritical, and proselytizing. While Christians have been busy defining themselves against one another, the broader culture looks on with disdain. Turned off largely by their own experiences with the church and inauthentic Christians they've known, many are rejecting organized religion altogether. To many onlookers, Christianity has become a parody of itself.

However, the most profound and unavoidable observation that confronted me as I answered Haley was how significantly Christianity had become divided and incoherent to the average spiritual sojourner. The century-long buildup to this perfect storm had wreaked havoc on the movement of Jesus. Many spiritually curious non-Christians weren't seeing a clear expression of God's work through Christians. Instead, they were experiencing splinters of a fractured community laden with dysfunction.

To clarify I went on to describe the different ways Christians interact with culture today by using labels representing the key mentalities that now dot the Christian landscape. I avoided the official terms delineating denominations or affiliation, knowing that would only further confuse the conversation. I stuck to the basics: What do they emphasize? How do they interact with the world? Where did this mentality come from?

I approached their whiteboard and began to draw.

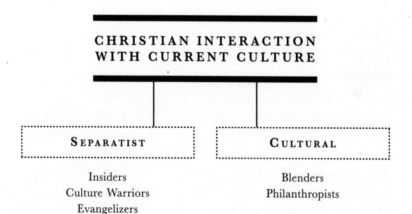

CHRISTIAN INTERACTION WITH CURRENT CULTURE

SEPARATIST	CULTURAL
Insiders	Blenders
Culture Warriors	Philanthropists
Evangelizers	

One by one, I described each category for her. When you first hear the descriptions I offered Haley, your tendency may be to disassociate from them. The groupings come from my conversations with both outsiders and Christians. They shine light on how the majority of Christians are reacting to our changing world. If you're honest, you'll likely find yourself representing one or more of these perspectives when engaging society. Take note and consider what can be learned by stepping back and seeing our faith the way our world does.

INSIDERS

Insiders earn their label from the spaces they choose to occupy—or perhaps the spaces they avoid at all costs. Their lives revolve primarily around "Christian" activities and functions involving other believers. From church basketball leagues to summer camps, these Christians spend the majority of their time in Christian communities—"safe" places. Their kids attend Christian schools, listen to Christian radio, and wear T-shirts on which well-known brands are replaced with Christian slogans. (Instead of a Facebook screen print, it says *"Faithbook:* what's your status?") You probably know the type.

Their motivation for retreating and separating from the broader culture can be attributed to a longing for purity, integrity, and holiness in life. But by default, their choice to live outside the typical rhythms of culture makes them seem awkward, disconnected, and judgmental toward others. As our research showed in *UnChristian,* 87 percent of young outsiders labeled Christians as judgmental. They feel that many Christians look down their noses at anyone different from them. This isn't surprising. Conventional logic asserts that if people think the world is predominantly evil, the wise choice is to remove themselves from it. When they do, their posture toward everyone else will likely be taken as disapproving.

Some take this separation and judgmental posture to an extreme. They come across as "holier than thou" and make mental lists of sins that, to them, are clearly wrong and unjustifiable for a "true Christian." Smoking, drinking, cussing, boys with earrings and tattoos, or even cutting your grass on Sunday might make it onto the list. They sincerely believe that anyone who participates in these activities couldn't possibly have a relationship with God. Strangely, gossip, gluttony, and materialism never make their list.

CULTURE WARRIORS

It was summer in the South. The temperatures were heating up, and the Alabama police braced themselves in the epicenter of the latest media circus. The clash over a 2.6-ton monument of the Ten Commandments in an Alabama courthouse was taking center stage.

On one side was Judge Roy Moore, who, in his own words, installed the monument to depict "the sovereignty of God over the affairs of men." By this, "the Chief Justice specifically meant the Judeo-Christian God of the Holy Bible and not the God of any other religion."[1] Supporting him were thousands of angry and frustrated Christians determined to make a valiant last stand in the culture war.

On the other side, proponents wanting the monument removed believed that "Roy's Rock" illegitimately aligned the American judicial system with Christianity to the exclusion of everything else. They stood proudly wrapped in sandwich boards, protest signs in hand, arguing for the separation of church and state.

The rallies and rhetoric escalated, with each side shouting

down the other while national media zoomed in on the battle. For weeks, national Christian radio personalities moved their audiences to see this as the front lines of the culture war. If the Ten Commandments stayed, then the Judeo-Christian public square would stay intact a little longer. If not, it was a sign that all hell was breaking loose, that the America known to Christians for centuries was falling apart at the seams. This was the defining moment.

Finally, the decision came down from the court. The monument was declared illegal inside the courthouse and orders were given for its immediate removal. The images saturated television news networks. Protesters were rabid.

As the rock was being pushed on a dolly out the doors of the state building, the news cut to an angry, emotional observer yelling at the top of his lungs: "Take your hands off my God!"[2]

Culture warriors, like the shouting man at the Alabama courthouse, often hold an underlying view that America and Christianity are deeply intertwined. They believe they have to take up proverbial arms against secularists who would pillage America's Christian heritage. These devoted followers regularly consume newsletters, radio shows, and magazines by Christian patriots, pastors, and pundits. If you happen across a culture warrior, you might be solicited to fight against the secularization of our nation and subjected to passionate pleas about moral decline. They are agitated to stand up for their moral convictions and vote for only pro-life and anti-gay-marriage politicians.[3] If you disagree with their cultural posture, beware. You might be labeled unpatriotic or worse . . . ungodly.

Culture warriors, many of whom are sincere and well intentioned, simply don't know how else to promote the ideals of their faith in the public square. Yet they are often unaware of how their tactics are perceived by others. This view motivates many of them—like the Roy's Rock angry supporter—to ensure that societal values and cultural artifacts reflect Christian beliefs. Even when society no longer behaves, thinks, or seeks the Christian God.

Don't get me wrong. Enrolling your kids in Christian school or tuning into Christian radio on your commute home from work doesn't necessarily make you holier-than-thou or judgmental. But when the faithful saturate their schedules with Christian events at Christian venues with Christian people, the world has a hard time believing we hold the rest of the world in high esteem.

EVANGELIZERS

Another group of Christians is intent solely on getting people "saved." To the evangelizer, recruiting others to the faith is the only *legitimate* Christian activity in the world. These Christians are motivated to "win souls for Christ," no matter who they offend. Wearing this calling like a chip on their shoulder, they might drop Jesus's name and the prospect of eternal damnation wherever they can get an audience.

Many evangelizers take seriously Old Testament Scripture that suggests that "blood will be on the hands" of those who neglect to share the good news.[4] Although some scholars argue that this is an incorrect interpretation of Scripture, evangelizers are compelled to save everyone they know. Their motivation is usually sincere and compassionate—but they don't always come off that way.

Take Bill, for instance. He was new to the neighborhood and enthusiastic about his latest career move. He was a respected

Christian leader recently recruited for the lead position at a large missions organization (a place that annually invests millions of dollars supporting missionary activities around the world). His family was making the transition to Atlanta's suburbs, and he was excited about opportunities a new city and fresh experiences might bring.

With Halloween arriving, it seemed like the perfect opportunity for Bill, an evangelism-focused Christian. Hundreds of children and families would be enthusiastically visiting his doorstep, looking only for M&M's and Reese's Peanut Butter Cups, but he would give them something more.

For the families on Bill's street, Halloween is always a community-wide event. The parents love the experience as much as the kids. They get a chance to hang out while their costumed children pillage house after house for their annual treasure. Everyone has a great time—a real community-bonding experience.

This year was no different and Halloween seemed to go off without a hitch.

But the next morning, there was a collective groan among the neighborhood moms. Comparing stories, they realized they'd all been duped. As their kids rummaged through their chocolate and gum, to a child they had each received a Gospel tract (a pamphlet that communicates the Christian faith).

The moms were appalled. As they put the evidence together, they discovered that Bill, the new guy, was the culprit. They were a bit surprised at the energy a neighbor would put into proselytizing their kids on Halloween night.

Bill is an evangelizer, and to be fair, he thought he was doing what was best. Driven by a desire to spread the "good news," he felt compelled to use any method possible. Thinking he was building bridges, he had actually accomplished the opposite. His plan to show love to his neighbors had backfired.

Bill's approach strikes me as ironic. Professionally, his mission was to take the message of Jesus to the world, but personally, he had turned every one of his own neighbors against him. His good intentions fell short of any real, substantive progress. He likely ruined his chances of having meaningful interaction with his new neighbors anytime soon.

This isn't only Bill's experience; it's symbolic of the way evangelizers interact with our world. While evangelism has always been a central part of the Christian mission, evangelizers see it as *the* most important or only interaction they can have in the world. For them, the ability, courage, and boldness to witness—in hopes of winning converts—is the defining mark of the truly faithful.[5]

*　*　*

AT THIS POINT, Haley was getting more than she had bargained for. I was only warming up. To simplify the situation a bit, I summed up the three types of Christian I had described so far—the insiders, culture warriors, and evangelizers. There was a common denominator they shared. They represented those whom I've come to call *Separatist Christians.*

Compelled to confront the world with their beliefs, Separatist groups play the antagonist, unconcerned about the social consequences of their tactics. They take seriously Jesus's call to bring their light into the world, even if it means judging (insiders), confronting (culture warriors), and proselytizing (evangelizers) those outside conservative Christian religion.

Separatist is a category familiar to me because it's the expression in which I was raised. When I was growing up, separation could have been our family motto. From kindergarten to high school graduation, I attended a private Christian school. Christian education was my parents' number one priority. They weren't always sure they could afford it, but it was so important that other financial needs would be sacrificed to make it happen.

My parents are two of the godliest people I know, and I don't resent my upbringing. I can remember coming downstairs early in the morning and seeing my mother and father reading the Bible and praying at the kitchen table together. They read their Bible and prayed every day—for them, it was *the* essential discipline of the Christian life. And consequently their lives reflect the most sincerity and integrity of anyone I've ever known. Whatever can be said about the choices they made in raising us, they certainly did not choose the easy road to following Jesus. I can only pray that I show my own children such depth of commitment, character, dependability, and faithfulness.

Yet I also realize the unintended consequence was instilling in me a belief that the role of a Christian was to be separate from the world. I often wonder how helpful it was to completely disconnect ourselves from the world's happenings around us. Families like ours who chose to separate from the world do so believing it is the only way to maintain their purity and holiness in a fallen, sinful place. This leads them to interact exclusively within their own circles, thus having very few meaningful relationships with people outside the subculture. Separatist Christians associate primarily with organizations that actually label themselves Christian, from youth basketball leagues to summer camps. These kinds of Christians are faithful church attendees and relentlessly committed to their principles. No one should question their spiritual devotion, but we might ask the question Is there a better way?

Ultimately, the Separatist Christian mentality is the remnant of the century-old Fundamentalist movement. Knowing this helps frame the dynamics at play. When the Christian faith became threatened near the beginning of the twentieth century by a secular-leaning society, leaders seized the opportunity to rally the troops. They treated these "secularizing forces within American culture at large," as the enemy, created an adversary, and then retreated behind their fortress of doctrinal statements. The entire movement has always been characterized by an *oppositionalist* mentality.

Although getting back to "the fundamentals of the faith" was their rally cry, combating a secular America seems to be their true objective. As the historian Alister McGrath says, "To treat fundamentalism simply as conservative religion confuses the characteristic and the distinctive."[6] It goes much deeper than that. Fundamentalism is "a countercultural movement that uses [doctrine] as a means of defining cultural boundaries . . . intended as much to alienate secular culture as to give fundamentalists a sense of identity and purpose."[7]

This clarifies how the Separatist expression of Christianity has become so vocal and dominant. As the culture grows more "godless," the Christians have a reason to circle the wagons. Caring little about any broader purpose in the world (other than seeking conversions), they shout their views *at* the world and huddle safely with each other—far away from a world they believe is literally going to hell.

* * *

AT THIS POINT, I was only halfway through my summary for Haley. There were two more groups that stand out among those sharing the Christian label that I felt she needed to know about.

BLENDERS

Blenders identify with the beliefs of Christianity on a spiritual level, but at the cultural level, they attempt to blend with the mainstream. In our research study for *UnChristian,* we asked young non-Christians whether they perceived the lifestyle of a Christian to be much different from their own. Of the 84 percent who knew a Christian personally, only 15 percent thought their lifestyles were any different.[8] Chances are, most of the Christian friends they referenced want to be seen as normal— and represent the classic blender mentality.

This group best reflects the next generation's values. Their lives mirror much of what everyone else is doing with little delineation between how they behave or what they believe. They are not all that interested in taking public stands for their convictions or faith; they think that's what the "crazy Christians" (the Separatists) do. Blenders have one concern: being like everyone else. They've seen how Christians who wear their faith on their sleeves have been alienated from the "in" crowd. They have no desire to go down that path. As far as they are concerned, serious discussion about religion is a taboo topic— off-limits for casual conversation.

My friend Dave grew up Catholic but never felt comfortable identifying himself with Christianity. Doing so would carry too much baggage. It was best to be avoided. One day we were having lunch and I asked him how he became Catholic. He told me outright, "My parents were Irish Catholic so I was born into it— that's just how it works."

This is a familiar story for many Christians. As we kept talking, Dave fondly recalled their Sunday-morning routine. They'd dress up for Mass and head to church, but look forward to post-Mass brunch the most. For Dave, church was a weekly event—a social opportunity for the family to spend time together doing something good. But it wasn't all fun. He recalled Sister Marie Reginald—the saint he still feared most to this day. She fit the classic nun stereotype, willing "to beat the hell out of 'em" with her ruler. From the look in his eyes, he'd received his fair share of knuckle raps!

For blenders, being Catholic (or Anglican, or Lutheran, etc.) isn't ever a choice; they just inherit their parents' religion—it's a generational hand-me-down. Most blenders are raised in a family where faith is part of their heritage. They likely attended church regularly at some season of their life (usually when they were younger), but their faith is a by-product of family identity, not always a personal decision.

Over the last decade, several churches—even evangelical ones—have responded to this "blender" mentality by accommodating their congregation's need to fit in. I've seen an increasing number of Protestant churches rearrange their entire method of doing church to suit this group under the banner of "relevance."[9]

At times, I've visited churches like these, so I understand the sincerity of the goal. Their highest value is to create an atmosphere of acceptance—which is definitely a Christ-like characteristic. On the surface, this seems to be admirable. They place emphasis on providing a comfortable environment where all are welcome. When they do, spiritual seekers and blenders feel right at home. Complete with a Starbucks-style coffee shop, Disney-like children's programming, and a worship experience that rivals a Coldplay concert, weekend services attempt to emulate the cultural competition.

To be fair, these churches *are* playing a part in helping some blenders take the role of faith in their life more seriously. Yet the critique of these churches is their neglect of historic church practices, like regular taking of the Eucharist (Communion) and emphasis on Bible teaching and personal disciplines like prayer and confession.

PHILANTHROPISTS

The final group of Christians I outlined for Haley was philanthropists. Putting an emphasis on doing good works is their defining mark. They serve in soup kitchens, clean garbage off the side of the highway, and help lead Boy Scout troops. One of their highest values is to make the world a better place. Some admit to enjoying a sense of earning God's approval through their efforts.

Of course, the Bible states explicitly that good works are integral to the Christian faith. James even writes that faith without works is dead.[10] But, for the philanthropists, these good activities often replace, rather than enhance, a deeper connection with Jesus. Oftentimes the Gospel gets lost in their work. In their pursuit of very great things, they forget the most important part of our faith. And although their work may be informed by the Gospel, it's not always explicitly communicated. You likely know a church like this. They are deeply involved in serving the needs of the communities, but if you were to ask someone in their church what Jesus means to them—you'd be met with an explanation of his good deeds. But what's missing is the compelling narrative of the Gospel from which all their good works emanate. Rather than root themselves in the precept that Jesus's gift of grace is freely offered with no strings attached, they seemingly attempt to prove their worth through acts of service and good deeds.

* * *

I SHOWED HALEY how these last two ways of Christians' interacting with the world had a pattern as well. Each was interested in being accepted—in fitting in with the current culture—and appalled at prospects of rocking the boat. That's not all bad. These Christians are usually very involved in their communities, volunteering at their children's public schools and, in many cases, providing stability for advancing the common good in American society today. The churches they attend often host community events, serve as voting precincts, and organize consignment sales for mothers in need of children's clothes.[11]

The label I give these two expressions—the blenders and the philanthropists—is *Cultural Christians*. They don't obsess about the afterlife and generally believe heaven is reserved for most everyone, except for the awful folks—like murderers, pedophiles, and men who don't pay child support. They can be credited with doing a lot of good in the world, but offer little in the way of distinction.

While Separatist Christians feel called away from the world, Cultural Christians conflate their faith with the culture itself. The problem here is that there has always been a certain "otherness" to our faith. The Gospel is a radical call to a stark existence, not a shallow assimilation.

Many of these Christians grew up in a mainline Protestant denomination or the Roman Catholic Church. But now they struggle to find any tangible benefit to their faith, except that they "fit in" to the bigger landscape of religion in America. Cultural Christians can also exist among the Presbyterians, Baptists, Pentecostals, and other sorts of evangelical groups. In a few geographical areas of the United States (like the Midwest or South), it's still acceptable, and perhaps even advantageous, to show up at church once in a while. Unfortunately, in these casual encounters with their so-called faith, the Christian call to Gospel-infused cultural engagement gets lost.

* * *

THE EXAMPLE MODELED by Jesus seems to offer a critique of these two broad attitudes—Separatist and Cultural Christians. The first-century world that rejected Christ struggled with the same expressions of faith.

In his culture, like ours, people of faith were struggling with how to respond to tremendous changes in their society. Their Jewish nation had fallen out of existence; they paid taxes to the Romans; they were bullied by Roman soldiers; they had to walk by the new Roman baths, theaters, and gymnasiums every day; they had to put up with the musings of Greek philosophers— even their holy Scripture was now written in Greek. They longed for the good ol' days when Israel was a nation. When, at will, they could exert their faith and overcome any challenge that confronted them.

Some Jews, called *Pharisees,*[12] believed that holiness—strict, rigid obedience to the Law of Moses and to all the traditions— was the only way to ride these bad times out. At the same time, another group called the *Essenes* was so disgusted by the immorality and impurity they saw that they decided to distance themselves from society and await God's return to Israel. They were reacting like the Separatists of today.

In contrast, the *Sadducees* and *Herodians* bore striking resemblance to the Cultural Christians. These two groups decided not to put up a fight with the societal changes taking place all around them. They determined it was better just to go along with culture and accommodate the change. They assumed that the faith to which they ascribed couldn't make much of a difference culturally; it should remain a private matter, a relic of their heritage. Their faith had become "cultural" in the truest sense.

Jesus's perspective appears to stand in stark contrast to both expressions. For the Separatist Pharisees and Essenes of his day—too concerned with purity and holiness when it came to associating with others—he flipped their belief on its head. The Pharisaic view had been "make yourself clean, and then you can eat with me." But Jesus modeled something altogether different: "Eat with me, and I will make you clean."[13] The biblical scholar Craig Blomberg calls Jesus's way of interacting "contagious holiness."[14] He writes:

> Jesus discloses not one instance of fearing contamination, whether moral or ritual, by associating with the wicked or impure. Rather, he believes that his purity can rub off on them, and he hopes that his magnanimity toward them will lead them to heed his calls to discipleship.[15]

Jesus also avoided the Cultural Christian mentality possessed by the Sadducees and Herodians. He didn't give in to the political pressure of the day to use the church as a place for merchants to set up shop. He charged into the temple and flipped over their tables—reminding them that the House of God was not a place for entertainment and consumerism.

Jesus lived, modeled, taught, and embodied a different way—a better way.

Little has changed.

But every now and then throughout history, there are moments when we are given the opportunity to step back; to recognize that the irreducible minimum for all Christians is Jesus. In light of this realization, we reevaluate where we sit and consider what God may be doing.

* * *

HALEY SEEMED TO have personal experience with just about every type of Christian I had described but intuitively felt that there must be more. She was right.

"Isn't there another type of Christian who is getting it right?" I was hoping she'd ask. I walked back to the whiteboard and drew one more line.

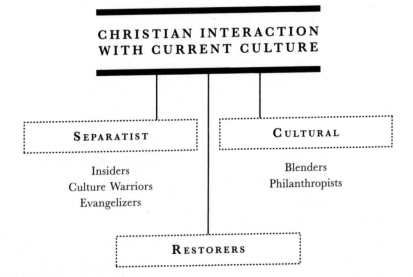

CHRISTIAN INTERACTION WITH CURRENT CULTURE

SEPARATIST
Insiders
Culture Warriors
Evangelizers

CULTURAL
Blenders
Philanthropists

RESTORERS

I began unfolding for her a third way of Christian expression that seemed to be emerging. Those who followed this third way were forging a new frontier and breathing life into the world.

RESTORERS

I've observed a new generation of Christians who feel empowered. Restorers exhibit the mind-set, humility, and commitment that seem destined to rejuvenate the momentum of the faith. They have a peculiar way of thinking, being, and doing that is radically different from previous generations. Telling others about Jesus is important, but conversion isn't their only motive. Their mission is to infuse the world with beauty, grace, justice, and love.

I call them restorers because they envision the world as it was meant to be and they work toward that vision. Restorers seek to mend earth's brokenness. They recognize that the world will not be completely healed until Christ's return, but they believe that the process begins now as we partner with God. Through sowing seeds of restoration, they believe others will see Christ through us and the Christian faith will reap a much larger harvest.

They are purposeful about their careers and generous with their time and possessions. They don't separate from the world *or* blend in; rather, they thoughtfully *engage*. Fully aware of the seachange under way, they are optimistic that God is on the move—doing something unique in our time.

They possess a way of following Jesus that is radically different from the others I've described. And they may carry the most hope for the future credibility of the entire Christian movement in the West. It combines the best of both expressions (both Separatist and Cultural Christians *do* have strengths) but adds an entirely new ingredient that makes their faith come alive: restoration.

The perspective they exhibit is not a new Christian idea; it's actually quite old. But what's fascinating to see is how they have latched onto one concept in particular and applied it in every area of their life. Their faith activity isn't restricted to "religious" activities, but carries over into every day of the week and each aspect of their careers, relationships, and social lives.

I finished my presentation at Lionsgate wondering if I had been of any help to Haley and her team. Perhaps my presentation forced me to organize these categories in my head more than it helped their team gear up for a new marketing campaign. The categories I gave her described how Christians in America were relating to culture in the midst of a seismic culture shift. I am sure they weren't perfect, but they expressed a sentiment about which I was convinced.

The way many were relating to culture had hurt our faith's image and, more important, impeded the Christian mission. But as a new generation was rising up, many of them were taking a different path. Determined not to become another punch line in the Christian parody, these faithful followers are committed to writing a compelling restorative narrative.

FOUR

Relearning Restoration

IN DECEMBER 1987, TOM WOLFE PENNED AN ARTICLE IN THE *American Spectator* titled "The Great Relearning." Wolfe, an acclaimed writer and cultural observer, contended that American life in the twentieth century had gone awry. Modern life was now defined by our arrogance "to defy the gods and try to push man's power and freedom to limitless, god-like extremes."[1] Americans had fallen under the spell that no problem was too big for science, technology, and innovation to solve. He boldly observed that we have forgotten many of the great lessons history taught us. We've traded in our collective intelligence—our learning passed down from generation to generation—for a blind pursuit of the new frontier.

He used an interesting metaphor to make his point. Citing a subgroup of the hippie movement in San Francisco, Wolfe explained how diseases like the mange, scroff, and rot reemerged in the 1960s. This subgroup had thrown off basic social restraints, like not sharing toothbrushes, not drinking from the same bottles, and not sleeping on the same sheets without washing them. To counteract the spread of these illnesses, they'd be forced to *relearn* the basic laws of personal hygiene.

As Wolfe explained, an epidemiological shift in the twentieth century pushed society to reacquaint themselves with foundational principles. Such is often the case, even outside the world of hygiene and health care. When culture changes, society rediscovers those ideals that have always grounded us.

In the midst of this great religious shift, Christians are following suit. Rather than relearning basic hygiene, Christians in the twenty-first century are relearning the comprehensive story of God. They are recovering the depth and the breadth of the most critical, orthodox teaching of our faith—the Gospel message. As the foundation of the Christian faith, God's story determines what we communicate to a wider society about who we are and what we think about the world. Interestingly, God's story is something many of us already know, or knew. Yet many Christians have forgotten parts of it or truncate it.

You're probably familiar with the typical presentation of the Gospel. It usually gets tacked on to sermons in the form of this fatal, somewhat fear-based question: "If you were to die tonight, would you spend eternity in heaven or hell?" After a dramatic pause, the pastor presents the Gospel like this: "You are a sinner bound for hell and Christ's death and resurrection can give you eternal life in heaven, if you'll just believe."

While you might quibble with a word or two or wish there was a better way to phrase it, this is the Gospel told by many American Christians. They believe it's the foundational assertion of the Bible—the driving motivation for everything they do. And this presentation of the Gospel is what invites the criticism.

The next Christians claim that the beginning (God's goodness throughout creation) and the ending (the restoration of all things) of the greater story have been conveniently cut out, leaving modern-day Christians with an incoherent understanding of the Gospel. Many are bound to a Gospel story with a climax that feels actually quite boring. "Go tell others how to escape from Planet Earth" doesn't feel like a compelling mission to them. Sure, they want to help others come to know the way of Jesus, but they believe their story should affect real lives and situations now. Not just in the afterlife.

Although technically accurate, the next Christians argue it misses the larger point. They suggest that this telling of the Gospel only includes half of God's story.[2] By truncating the full narrative, it reduces the power of God's redeeming work on the cross to just a proverbial ticket to a good afterlife. *Is this all there is to Christianity? Did Jesus die only so we could get out of this place and go somewhere else?*

While the redemptive Christ event is the apex of the story, it isn't the whole story. The story begins in the context of a perfect garden and continues through God's promise of restoration. We can't cut the branch of redemption off the tree of God's story and whittle it to fit our purposes. Creation and restoration are the bookends to Christ's earthly work and they are shaping how the next Christians holistically participate in the world.

THE PROBLEM WITH HALF STORIES

God's story is made up of four key parts: creation, fall, redemption, restoration (and ultimately consumation). The truncated Gospel that is often recounted is faithful to the fall and redemption pieces of the story, but largely ignores the creation and restoration components. These missing elements are at the heart of what a new generation of Christians are relearning, and subsequently, retelling.

From the very beginning of Scripture, Christians are introduced to a God who calls his creation "very good." Genesis poetically tells the story of God breathing life into humans and forming them in his own image (the *imago dei*). Knowing God's image exists in every human being explains why all of us—not just Christians—know how to love and be generous, creative, kind, and caring. As people naturally seek to know where they've come from and what they were made to enjoy, the good design of creation explains a lot. For one thing, creation shows us how things ought to be. Our fascination with beauty, hunger for relationships, bent toward goodness and justice, and longing for connection with a transcendent God are all clues about our origins.[3] Consider the innocence, idealism, and bigger-than-life dreams that come so easily to children. These ideas are hard-wired into every individual made in God's image (Gn 1:26–27).

Half-story versions begin abruptly in Genesis 3, where the separation of humanity from God is the opening scene. This story starts with everyone as corrupted sinners, with little rationalization given for non-Christians who still do good works. All the evidence suggests that this version of the story isn't connecting with the next generation. It not only begins with a judgmental tone but also seems to miss some element of truth postmodern seekers have experienced—namely the human compulsion to do good.

Acknowledging there was goodness in the beginning doesn't eliminate corruption from the story; it just starts the story in a more foundational place. We all see corruption playing out around us. In my own life, I feel it when I dominate relationships with power instead of love or unwittingly poison friendships with self-centeredness and egotistical defaults instead of

service and humility. I see it in the lives of friends whose mar-
riages are destroyed by their unconquerable draw to pornography or career advancement. No one is immune to poor choices.
As Michael Metzger wrote, "Our consciences, callings, art, ethics, responsibility, family and marriage, health, history, imagination, kingdom, culture and society, work, ecology, angelic
realms, academics, leisure and rest, worship, sexuality and language are stained by the sin of the original couple."[4] That's why
Christ came, to satisfy our sin debt so that we could experience
a new way of living: restoration.

The next Christians believe that Christ's death and Resurrection were not only meant to save people *from* something. He
wanted to save Christians *to* something. God longs to restore
his image in them, and let them loose, freeing them to pursue
his original dreams for the entire world. Here, now, today, tomorrow. They no longer feel bound to wait for heaven or spend
all of their time telling people what they should believe. Instead, they are participating with God in his restoration project
for the whole world.

They recognize that Christ's redemptive work is not the end
or even the goal of our stories; redemption is the beginning of
our participation in God's work of restoration in our lives and
in the world. Understanding that one idea literally changes everything.

Books by the scores have flooded the market giving perspective to this new way of thinking. Authors like Dallas Willard,
Brennan Manning, Scot McKnight, Chuck Colson, N. T. Wright,
Michael Metzger, Todd Hunter, Nancy Pearcey, Chris Seay,
Lauren Winner, Tim Keller, and Richard Stearns are offering
new viewpoints on the whole story of God. Among other things,
these thinkers realize that the beginning of the story must

begin at the beginning and continue into this very moment in time.

*   *   *

THE STORY BEGINS in a garden that God himself planted. It's beautiful and bountiful, and human beings flourish there. God wanted the human encounter of their world to be marked by elegance, simplicity, and beauty—recognizing it was purposed and intentioned to be something great. It obviously isn't that way anymore, but in its original state the creation was good, *really* good. No violence, no conflict, and no deceit. Peace, harmony, and beauty prevailed.

Utopia wouldn't last. A serpent tempts the first couple to disobey God and pursue their own interests. Suddenly, perfection is corrupted and humans come into conflict with the world, God, and each other. Thistles began to grow on flowers, and harvests suddenly required work. People began to pursue selfish relationships, and humans no longer walked alongside God. The world broke.

Even in the garden, however, God made a promise that brokenness wouldn't reign forever. In Genesis 3:15, a promise is made that one day a rescuer would ride in to repair the corruption. Scholars refer to this foretelling as the "proto-evangelium" or "Gospel beginning." In the shadow of a good garden, we feel the first tremors of Christ's coming.

He promised that eventually sin and destruction and death would be defeated. All humans could do was wait. Hundreds of years passed as God worked miracles among his people. He delivered them from cruel slave masters, and gave them a new bountiful land. He helped them defeat enemies, sent them prophets to guide them, and brought peace to their communities.

As humans often do, God's people grew selfish and stubborn. They forgot their Deliverer, and God responded with silence. Until one day, he shattered the silence when Jesus Christ was born in Israel. His life becomes an impeccable example of what it means to image God. Every moment of his ministry is spent with the poor, sick, helpless, and hurting. Traveling from place to place, Christ leaves a wake of healing and restoration.

His ministry was cut short, however, as he offered himself up as a self-described sacrifice for humanity. The evil that flooded the world in the beginning would again rear its head. Fulfilling Isaiah's prophecies, Jesus brings peace to humanity's corruption through suffering servanthood by paying for all the sins that had rippled from the garden to Golgotha. Dying on a cross, he begins to turn back the bad deeds done in the good garden, and through his Resurrection he begins a new age of hope on earth.

Two thousand years after the Christ event, people are still on earth and the hope is not diminished. Paul tells us in Colossians 1, that Christ's shed blood began a restorative work affecting the eternal things of heaven as well as the here and now events on earth. More than simply offering us a postmortem destination, God commissioned us to share his whole story and become conduits for him to bring healing to earth and its residents. Like a capstone to the story of God, Christians are called to partner in a restorative work so that the torch of hope is carried until Christ returns.

This is the story of God.

The whole story.

God's story begins with a perfect creation and methodically winds through history bringing us to Jesus and inaugurating our here-and-now mission. This story doesn't fit neatly on the end of a sermon, but it seems to carry a little more weight.

*   *   *

MY WIFE, REBEKAH, loves to read fiction. When she was growing up, her life revolved around reading. From Laura Ingalls
Wilder's Little House series to Encyclopedia Brown and Nancy
Drew, she could always be found curled up, book in hand,
oblivious to the rest of the world. When Rebekah finally learned
to drive, she had trouble finding her family's church. Her head
had been buried in books in the backseat of the car for a decade.

Great stories have this effect on us—whether in literature,
theater, film, or pop culture. They draw us into their world to
play with our emotions and manipulate our imagination. From
The Brothers Karamazov and *Les Miserables* to *Lord of the Rings* and
Twilight, good stories have a certain power. Their compelling
characters have dreams, temptations, and heartaches that we
can identify with. Good stories usually resolve conflict and fulfill
our hopes of a heroic outcome. A story without these elements
feels flat and usually leaves us dissatisfied, which might give us a
clue to why a new generation of Christians get frustrated with
the abridged version of God's epic encounter with humanity.

Explaining the Gospel as a half-story to a spiritual seeker
would be the equivalent of giving Rebekah a James Patterson
novel with the first and last hundred pages removed. It would
be incomplete and make little sense. Left with no real story at
all, Rebekah would be frustrated and confused. She'd have no
context and no conclusion. Furthermore, it would disrespect
Patterson, who took time to craft those parts of the story for his
readers.

I don't mean to diminish the importance of telling others
about God's redemption accomplished on the cross, and we
shouldn't deny that salvation through faith in Jesus has eternal

implications. But shouldn't we be faithful to recount and live out the whole story?

RESTORATION UNTIL THE END

Few places are more beautiful than Carmel, California, in the spring. Situated on the cliffs overlooking a marine reserve in the Pacific Ocean sits a private estate called the James House. Occasionally, I get the opportunity to host gatherings for our organization there. It's one of my favorite places on earth.

On one particular weekend, it served as the perfect backdrop for the conversations we were having. Our guests were influential leaders throughout American society who embody the very idea of restoration that we've only just begun to uncover. Among those participating were magazine editors, White House liaisons, bestselling authors, Grammy-winning songwriters, ecocommerce entrepreneurs, nation-building diplomats, fashion photographers, and founders of some of the most influential nongovernmental organizations in the world. I am humbled by the opportunity to host this type of gathering a few times a year. It's central to the mission of our organization. I enjoy introducing innovators to one another and encouraging them to collaborate on various projects addressing a variety of global concerns.

Not only is this estate a breathtaking place to be, but it has its own storyline that is deeply symbolic of this great shift occurring in the next Christians.

Sculpted out of the side of a sixty-foot-tall coastal cliff, the James House was once the prize of Carmel. Built by famous American architect Charles Greene, the design and intention of every detail is spectacular. In the early 1900s, he instructed his builders to place the home's foundation in the bedrock of the cliff—some forty-five feet below the floor level of the home (never mind that it added four years to its completion date). He was intent on ensuring it would stand the test of time, the ocean surf, the wind, and the rain—almost daily occurrences on the northern California coast.

Situated above the Point Lobos Marine Sanctuary, you can tell this beautiful estate was built to portray an image of Eden. Flowers bloom year-round, pathways are handcrafted from stone, green meadows glisten from the spray of the ocean mist—the foresight, design, and plans for this mansion were almost perfect.

Several generations after its completion and the death of its owner, the house fell into disrepair. For years, a widow lived in a corner bedroom of this 3,500-square-foot castlelike habitat. Walls were crumbling, and the roof leaked. Hidden by a tall fence, no one knew what had come of the estate. It was just as well. Just a few miles north, the rest of Carmel had been developing quite nicely, so little attention was paid to its decline.

Then, several years ago, a man named Joe came along.

As an insightful investor, he had the eyes to see what *could* be. He was experienced at seeing opportunity and potential, even in dire situations. A career in the financial markets had given him keen insight into knowing where latent potential rests. And this piece of property was screaming for attention.

After purchasing the estate, Joe began the intentional pursuit of restoring it. Hundreds of man hours went into the arduous task of removing overgrown brush, trash, and debris. Scraping away the refuse from years of neglect and abandonment was a painstaking chore. After months of hard work, it was finally ready.

Reconstruction on the home could begin.

But Joe didn't want to bring just his *new* vision to the property; he wanted to go back to the old. He wanted to restore the home to what the original designer intended. This is the way he believed the home ought to be. Through dedicated research, Joe uncovered the letters between the architects and the estate's original owner. Clues about their grandest hopes and expectations for this property peppered the correspondence.

Laborious work went into every detail of the restoration. He refinished the rounded corners on the doors and the rough plastered walls—ensuring every shadow from the setting sun cast only soft lines. He had the red baked tile roof completely repaired and the gardens manicured to perfection. Even the seagulls were rediscovering a place to roost.

His work didn't stop there. In the years since, Joe has continued to improve on the original design of this property. He used the footprint from the dilapidated beginnings of a greenhouse to construct a magnificent one using recycled timber from old convents in Tasmania. He commissioned the Japanese artist Izumi to sculpt a five-ton stone and create a "sending and receiving" stream as an invitation to the grounds. These improvements are amazing, but it was the idea of restoring it to the planner's original intent that gave the project soul.

The idea of restoration is critical in the next Christian discussion. If you don't understand restoration, you won't understand the next Christians. They see themselves on a mission, partnering with God to breathe justice and mercy and peace and compassion and generosity into the world. They believe that in small ways they are turning back the hands of time to give the world a glimpse of what the world looked like before sin entered the picture. Like Joe, restoration fuels them to get to work.

Consider the discouragement for Christians when *restoration*—the "last hundred pages"—is removed from God's story. According to this version, the only meaningful role a believer can play is evangelism, either through doing it or supporting it. But this version of the Gospel runs the risk of leaving some Christians in the pew feeling disconnected. More important, it leaves many with no clear way to understand the restoration mandates throughout the New Testament. We all agree that evangelism is an important part of the life of the believer, but a truncated Gospel doesn't seem to fully utilize some appendages in the body of Christ.

Is evangelism really the only use for the millions of churchgoers in our culture?

Now, put restoration back into the story. Instantly, you've created millions of jobs for all the "unemployed" and bored Christians in the church—jobs they can get excited about. Now there is work to do for people who want to make the world a better place in the meantime. Instead of simply waiting for God to unveil the new heaven and the new earth, the rest of us can give the world a taste of what God's kingdom is all about—building up, repairing brokenness, showing mercy, reinstating hope, and generally adding value. In this expanded model, everyone plays an essential role. In this way, relearning becomes exciting and personal.

The bottom line is this: The next wave of Christian engagement seems inherently linked to this idea of restoration. The people who are shaping this movement believe with all their hearts that God is in the restoration business—not just in the afterlife, but here on earth as well. "Your kingdom come, your will be done, on earth as it is in heaven" (Mt 6:10). They consider restoration to be God's trademark, and they want to make it a central theme of the Christian faith again.[5]

THE POWER OF THE OUGHT

The morning sun was begging me to go for a run. I rose early—still on East Coast time—and decided to take a jogging tour of Stanford University's campus. The dew sat heavy on the blades of the freshly mowed grass. Crape myrtles were in bloom with fresh buds spewing pink all over the curb. The air at first light was a bit cool, but seemed filtered and purified, at least compared to the steady dose of smog I'd grown used to in Atlanta. On days like this, a two-mile run easily becomes four. I was feeling good, glad to be alive and eager with anticipation for what the rest of the day held.

Although a bit unsure of how the discussion would go, I knew the topic was significant. Invited to the Hoover Institution by George Shultz, President Reagan's former secretary of state, I had flown across the country for a meeting with thirty other leaders to discuss the topic "What should the Christian position be on nuclear weapons in a post–Cold War era?"

I must admit, I hadn't done much homework on the nuclear issue beyond some very basic, peripheral reading. Thanks to my busy schedule, the prereadings for this gathering never quite made it into my satchel. I'd really never considered what nuclear weapons had to do with my faith. It seemed best left to heads of state, national security advisers, and the military. I'd soon understand the connection.

One of the people present was Ambassador Max Kampelman, a Jewish conscientious objector during World War II. What's staggering about Max's story is the decision of service he made to his fellow man. Instead of going off to war, he faithfully fulfilled his draft obligation by participating in the legendary

Minnesota Starvation Experiment.[6] For an excruciating eleven months, he subjected himself to the physical rigor of controlled starvation all to help wartorn Europe learn how to restore health to those suffering from extreme starvation under the brutal force of the Gestapo. Max's body whittled away, but his spirit did the opposite. Instead of letting his mental sharpness fade like some of the others, he intentionally leveraged this period of time to pursue a law degree, which paved the way for him to serve as an ambassador in the Reagan administration decades later.

Meeting eighty-eight-year-old Max humbled me. He was five feet eight and wiry thin with hearing aids in both ears, but when he entered the room, proudly wearing his red and yellow "Hoover" tie, his presence commanded respect. In just eight minutes that day, he delivered a speech that still rings in my ears. With conviction in his voice and poise in his eyes, Max persuaded the assembly that they had only one option: to eliminate nuclear weapons from the face of the earth.

To most of us in the room, that seemed impossible. But Max saw the world differently. And that day, with a moral authority few can claim, he said something profound that crystallizes the restoration theme we've seen in the next Christians.

"We must recognize the power of the 'ought.' It's the power to change the world! We can't just see the world in terms of how it *is* today, or we will always feel defeated," he said passionately. "But when we see the world in terms of *how things ought to be*, we can dream for the impossible—and work to see it become reality."

What Max didn't realize was that in just five words—"*how things ought to be*"—he had sung the next Christians' anthem. They think, believe, live, and see the world in terms of fighting for how things ought to be. It's synonymous with their commitment to renewing and restoring all things. And this "how things ought to be" way of thinking harkens back to God's original intentions for the human soul and the world. It connects restoration to God's original intention in the garden.[7]

For the next Christians, the *ought* is the prism through which they see their mission. This includes sharing the Gospel so that men and women might enter into relationship with God, but it also goes beyond that. In the good garden there was no sickness or evil or pain. So these Christians set out to identify hurts, sickness, darkness, and evil, and then show up as a force of help, healing, and goodness. They have purposed to loose the strings of brokenness and set free God's intention.

*   *   *

At the age of twenty-seven, "Cat" (as her friends affectionately call her) had reached the pinnacle of her career. She was a Wall Street investor who had taken the venture capital world by storm, so you can imagine why she felt a little out of place when a friend invited her to tour "a correctional facility" in Texas. (In the Lonestar State, that's slang for a full-fledged prison that you wouldn't wish on your worst enemy.) Being free-spirited and adventurous, Cat accepted the invitation. She had no idea how much her life as a high-powered business executive was about to be turned upside down.

When she arrived at the prison, Cat realized that this was not going to be just another field trip. Walls decorated with barbed wire surrounded a towering facility that seemed to scream "Keep out." The only missing element was the banjo-playing man from *Deliverance*.

As she walked the aisle between cells exchanging glances with the inmates, her preconceptions began to fracture. Instead of seeing "wild, caged animals," she sensed unlimited possibility. Instead of hardened criminals, she met children without fathers and guilt-ridden men. Hopelessness seemed to reign in their expressions. Many inmates fit the classic profile of a sinner in need of salvation—that was obvious. But more than this, Cat could see something most others never did—glimmers of God's image radiating from their eyes. Instead of seeing the situation as it was, she had trained her mind to see things as they *ought* to be.

As a venture capitalist, she was one of the best at spotting raw business talent. Usually it came in the form of a future CEO presenting a three-hundred-plus-page business plan. Today it was showing up on the prison yard. In a moment of inspiration, Cat recognized that most criminals are really just great entrepreneurs acting as CEOs in an underground world. In their past, they've had to be good at recruitment, buying low and selling high, creating distribution channels, and managing their competition. Granted, most applied their skills in all the wrong places—like theft and unsophisticated drug dealing—but even in those instances they inherently understood key business concepts such as risk management and profitability. It's the way the criminal mind works.

She got excited imagining what could happen if inmates who were committed to their own transformation were equipped to start and run legitimate companies. What if she could convince seasoned executive leaders throughout corporate America to unearth the buried abilities possessed by convicted felons?

Motivated by the power of the *ought* to change lives, Cat launched a business plan competition in the middle of a Texas State prison. To her surprise, over fifty-five inmates enrolled.

She recruited fifteen world-class executives to tutor, mentor, and coach her new protégés through the process. Within just nine months, these inmates were wearing caps and gowns for graduation—proudly displaying their hard-earned diplomas from the Prison Entrepreneurship Program (PEP). With a little imagination, a sensitivity to notice something broken, and the courage to try to fix it, she was able to start what has become one of the most successful prisoner rehabilitation programs in the country.

Since 2005, PEP has not been just a feel-good story. The prisoners' hard work has produced staggering results in Texas. Fewer PEP graduates return to prison than other prisoners, and state prison officials continually laud their efforts. Cat has put to work her belief that "rebuilding the human spirit not only deters crime; it enhances society as a whole."[8] Her example illustrates how the next Christians are remaking the world for the better.[9]

Catherine's work illustrates the next Christian mind-set. She demonstrates the power of the ought at work. By looking back to the garden as a model for the future, restoration living can flood and transform our entire cosmos. With the ought pulsing through their veins, the next Christians are partnering with God to restore every corner of the earth.

THE JOURNEY AHEAD

Cat isn't the only Christian who operates in this framework. In the past few years, I've encountered hundreds just like her. They are scattered all across America and many of them don't even know that the others exist; yet they all follow a similar pattern.

The restorers I'll introduce you to in the coming pages don't simply act differently; their actions are driven by an entirely different set of ideas about *why* they restore. They aren't only concerned with helping broken people—they see an all-encompassing vision in which restoration fuels everything they do. It permeates every part of their being.

The way things ought to be becomes the driving mechanism behind

Why they care
Why they show up
Where they work
Who they spend time with
When they speak
And more important, when they shut up

This way of thinking doesn't necessarily make their lives easier. As T. S. Eliot reminds us, "When the Christian faith is not only felt, but thought, it has practical results which may be inconvenient."[10] And, let's be honest, following Jesus can be inconvenient.

The inconvenience is worth it to the next Christians because they desperately want the world to know the story of Jesus and the power of our faith. It starts with *rediscovering* the full story of the Gospel, which leads them to *recalibrate* their conscience to allow them to be in the world, which forces them to *rethink* their commitment to one another and their neighbors, which inspires them to *reimagine* a renaissance of creativity, beauty, and art that the world hasn't seen in centuries, which culminates in *redeploying* the church where the world needs it most. You can see how embracing restoration as part of God's story sets off a chain reaction that can *revitalize* our faith in the post-Christian century.

This collective of ideas represents a vision for a whole new way of being, living, and interacting that current generations have yet to experience. Up to this point, I've spoken in general terms about the landscape of rising generations. However, the chapters that follow attempt to zoom in on ought-minded restorers who live what I've been describing. I want to wrap these generalities in flesh by pairing common qualities of the next Christians with real-life stories of people who embody them.

The six characteristics that set apart the next Christians are that they are

Provoked, not offended
Creators, not critics
Called, not employed
Grounded, not distracted
In community, not alone
Countercultural, not "relevant"

The next Christians often show up where you least expect, in every channel of culture and every sphere of social interaction. From college suites, concerts, and entrepreneurial start-ups to social networking destinations and work. These Christians will show up in their schools, participate in volunteer programs, support civic government, read medical research, be proponents for a just prison system, plant community gardens, be patrons of art festivals and local coffee shops. They will be the most enthusiastic about human rights campaigns, interreligious dialogue, and will be known on the streets of their neighborhoods. You'll begin to recognize the restorers in your own life and perhaps discover that this way of being Christian is what you've been longing for.

When Christians incorporate these characteristics throughout the fabric of their lives, a fresh, yet orthodox way of being *Christian* springs forth. The death of yesterday becomes the birth of a great tomorrow and the end of an era becomes a beautiful new beginning. In this way, the end of Christian America becomes good news for Christians.

PART II
THE RESTORERS

FIVE

Provoked, *Not Offended*

AT NINETEEN, RENEE WAS NO STRANGER TO PAIN. SHE HAD become entangled in a drug addiction and was a victim of sex-. ual abuse. On one particular Florida night, she is high on pot, painkillers, alcohol, and cocaine. She shares a house in a rough part of town with friends who provide all the wrong influences. In a moment of desperation, she reaches out to another group of friends—Christians she once knew who always treated her differently. She's frantic for help, hope, and a new start.

Enter Jamie Tworkowski. He's a classic twenty-something hip-ster: single, clean-cut, artistic, with piercing brown eyes. Jamie is a Hurley Surf representative from Orlando who also happens to be a Christian. He doesn't pretend to have all the answers to life's toughest questions, but Jamie is convinced that *following Jesus is about restoring the broken.* His heart is bent that way and he follows its lead. Throughout most of his short life, Jamie has found himself on the listening end of some of the most brutal conversations about loss, pain, and loneliness. This particular night is no different.

On the bottom floor of Renee's home, with hell raining down above them, Jamie and friends listen, pray, and plead with her to get help.

She commits to going to rehab the next morning but asks for just one more night. They struggle to leave, but honor her request.

When Renee's front door closes, the double doors of her desperation swing wide open. With hot tears streaming down her face, Renee's fingers run for an old razor blade.

After fifty previous cuttings, one more scar wouldn't matter. Locked in a bathroom, she carves "F-U-C-K-U-P" across her left forearm. In case there is any question, she makes it clear to everyone what she believes about herself.

The next morning, Jamie and his friends pick Renee up. With her bandaged, bloodied arm, they arrive at a small clinic to get her help. Once again, she experiences ultimate rejection. The nurse discovers Renee's wound and realizes how deep the drugs are in her system. The resource-strapped clinic isn't equipped to handle her detox and turns her away. She's "too great a risk."

That night, their mission of love deepens. Jamie and friends become her immediate rehabilitation plan, filling prescriptions for basic human compassion, acceptance, and grace. In Jamie's words, "For the next five days, she was ours to love. We became her hospital and the possibility of healing filled our living room with life. It was unspoken and there were only a few of us, but we would be her church, the body of Christ coming alive to meet her needs, to write love on her arms."[1]

And love they did.

Inspired by Jesus's example, they offered Renee guerrilla-style rehab. She needed love and true friends. She needed to be on the receiving end of the Christian's responsibility to care, to show up in the darkest of places alongside other human beings in need. Lots of cigarettes, love, music, listening, all-nighters, Starbucks, and time pushed her back from the ledge.

Truth be told, many Christians would have been offended at Renee's lifestyle, disgusted at the "friends" who fed her addictions, and exasperated by her continual string of poor choices. *Renee doesn't care about anyone else; why should we care about her?*

Jamie wasn't offended that she had pilfered drugs for years while he had pursued a respectable career. He wasn't judgmental about the opportunities to turn her life around she had wasted. He could have condemned her, blown her off, prayed for her, or called someone else in to help—all while avoiding meaningful contact because of the negative toxicity of her situation. Instead, Jamie was provoked to engage; he rolled up his sleeves and got involved in the messy work of restoration.

Jamie represents the next Christians I've come to know in the past few years. His life embodies this revolutionary idea.

Jamie is a textbook *restorer*. He sees brokenness and seeks out ways to address it. He spots darkness and shows up with whatever light he can bring. No one would accuse Jamie of being judgmental. He is full of grace, giving the recipient of his love the benefit of the doubt. Looking for the best in people, he sees the image of God in everyone he encounters, even when their darker side gets the best of them.

I've seen this restoration way of thinking and living define a new generation of Christians in our world. They simply can't help themselves; they are intoxicated with the idea that God's love extends to all people. They believe this kind of love is expressed best in tangible, physical acts of goodness. They show up. In fact, showing up is *their* defining practice. These Christians don't run from areas that might typically offend a Separatist Christian—they run to them. They seek out brokenness and offer hope.

Christians like Jamie don't just get involved with the down-and-out. They put emphasis on carrying that mind-set into the larger cosmopolitan culture of the West. Even amid influential careers, they can be seen leveraging their influence for the benefit of others.

The next Christians stand up for what they deem to be good, true, and beautiful.

They have a deep respect for God's creations and strive to bring out that divine potential when most would write them off.

They are the fashion models who decline offers to do topless photo shoots, not because they are offended, but because they support the dignity of women.

They are business executives in the carbon industry who display "marketplace grace" by intentionally doing business with those who exhibit character and operate from deeper values than simply profit.

I've seen this play out in the story of a filmmaker who rejects a producer's attempt to make her script more crass simply to cash in on a target audience. She thinks differently, believing that how she tells her story through film should ultimately reflect her restoration mind-set.

It's the mom who plants a garden or mills her own wheat, knowing these intentional, time-sacrificing choices provide her family with the best possible health and helps preserve the remnant goodness in God's creation.

Or the college student who volunteers their time to tutor struggling classmates.

The next Christians shy away from framing their work in "Christian" terms. They are deeply committed, but equally wise. They understand the perceptions that exist about their faith and distinctly live out something different.

They proactively engage in our world, but not always the way their parents did.

OFFENDED AND WITHDRAWN

No one—Christians included—can avoid all contact with potentially corrupting people, systems, perspectives, and influences. For everyday followers of Jesus, this tension begs the question: How should Christians react when placed in an environment that celebrates sin, overlooks injustice, or tolerates immorality?

Michael Metzger has said, "When confronted with the corruption of our world—Christians ought to be provoked to engage, not offended and withdrawn."[2]

In contrast, classic Separatist Christians (the insiders, culture warriors, and evangelizers) are often offended by corruption. Characterized by their lifestyle choices, these Christians tend to remove themselves from potentially harmful situations—citing their disgust of immorality or their pursuit of holiness as the reason. As is consistent with their perspective, they condemn, judge, withdraw, and boycott. They play the paradoxical role of antagonist instead of the sacrificial pursuer.

This approach does little to transform our existing culture *or* further the mission of God in our world.

When a community is provoked, they assume a *proactive* posture; when a community is offended, they assume a *reactive* posture. Additionally, the restorers point out that a reactive posture was not the pattern of Jesus. When he was about thirty years old, Jesus began his public ministry in Israel. Around the same time, the Pharisees dominated the religious landscape. As I mentioned earlier, the Pharisees were known as the most holy and God-fearing Jews in the land. They emerged as a group many decades before the time of Jesus with the noble intention of preserving Judaism amid the corrupting influence of Greek culture. Over time, however, they became secluded and elitist. They focused on rigidly keeping the law and oral traditions that, for them, delineated the holy from the unholy, the good Jew from the unrighteous heathen. Thus, the Pharisees worked hard to dress different, to walk on the opposite side of the road when someone with sickness or an ailment was coming their way, and to set up boundary upon boundary to avoid corruption at all costs. Their response to culture was one of offense.

How did the Pharisees ever get to this place? Remember, they started with the right intentions: seeking obedience to God's commands in an atmosphere of cultural patterns and behaviors that were growing increasingly contrary to those commands (sound familiar?). I think Eugene Peterson's explanation is particularly helpful.

> Imagine yourself moving into a house with a huge picture window overlooking a grand view across a wide expanse of water enclosed by a range of snow-capped mountains. . . . Several times a day you interrupt your work and stand before this window to take in the majesty and the beauty. . . . One afternoon you notice some bird droppings on the window glass, get a bucket of water and a towel, and clean it. . . . Another day visitors come with a tribe of small dirty-fingered children. The moment they leave you see all the smudge-marks on the glass. They are hardly out the door before you have the bucket out. . . . Keeping that window clean develops into an obsessive-compulsive neurosis. You accumulate ladders

and buckets and squeegees. You construct a scaffolding both inside and out to make it possible to get to all the difficult corners and heights. You have the cleanest window in North America—but it's now been years since you looked through it. You've become a Pharisee.[3]

PROVOKED TO ENGAGE

In this context Jesus came and exposed the shortcomings of the Pharisees' response to the dirtiness and darkness of our world. Story after story in the Gospel accounts reveal God's heart for the lost, the down and out, for those who were "dirty." Jesus wasn't offended by their actions or broken lives; he was provoked to engage them. He sought them out to find a way to restore them both physically and spiritually.

Zacchaeus was a Jewish tax collector who collected Roman taxes from fellow Jews. He would skim off the top at their expense; he became rich while others struggled. As a result, Zacchaeus was perceived as a corrupt traitor. He was the lowest of the low—think Bernard Madoff. But Jesus was not offended by Zacchaeus or his unconscionable career. Jesus was drawn to him and even invited himself over to Zacchaeus's house for dinner—an intimate proposition to someone many considered the "chief of sinners" (Lk 19).

Or take the woman at the well (Jn 4). There were several reasons for a Jewish rabbi like Jesus to avoid her: She was a woman (strike one; Jewish rabbis did not converse with women when alone), she was a Samaritan (strike two; Jews hated Samaritans), and she was sexually promiscuous (strike three; no explanation needed). But Jesus engaged her.

What about the Roman centurion (Lk 7)? A Roman! A centurion! He represented everything that Jews detested about the Roman occupation. And yet Jesus healed his servant and praised his faith.

Or the Syrian-Phoenician woman (Mk 7)? She was a Gentile, and yet Jesus healed her daughter.

Or the man with leprosy (Mt 8)? He was unclean, yet Jesus engaged him and cured him.

Or the woman caught in adultery (Jn 8)? She was actually caught in the very act.[4] Jesus refused to judge her.

Jesus didn't seem to care how the religious viewed these people. He showed up anyway.

Sinners loved Jesus. They literally followed Jesus everywhere. They pursued him from town to town. He spent days with them, meeting their friends, eating meals in their homes, accepting their gifts, and embracing their children. They were suspended in disbelief at encounters with someone who understood truth and beauty, healing and restoration, righteousness, justice, mercy, and grace—and He *genuinely* loved them.

The self-righteous Pharisees were displeased. They didn't understand why Jesus would associate with such immoral people. But Jesus didn't just act differently: He thought differently. He saw people differently. He reminded them that he had come "to find and *restore* the lost."[5]

A NEW MIND-SET

This restoration mind-set guided Jesus's entire ministry. He was driven to be present in the darkest and most corrupt places of his culture, to extend his own holiness, love, grace, peace, and purity to others in creative, redemptive, and ultimately self-sacrificial ways. This is why God became a man in Jesus Christ. God's holiness did not prevent him from entering our messy depravity; it provoked him to show up.

This mentality will raise serious concerns. Engaging more with people, ideas, and environments that counter some of their greatest convictions and threaten to rattle their own faith can be disconcerting for some Christians.

These unavoidable dangers do not keep the next Christians from engagement; they do not withdraw behind their castle walls. Their depth of intimacy with Christ gives them a charitable mind-set that produces outward compassion toward others. It causes them to take seriously the commandment to love their neighbors, wherever they are. Cultural influences can be powerful. We've all seen friends struggle when they allow unhealthy environments to seep into their being and reshape their beliefs and values. Acting on this "restoration" perspective can create the dangerous potential to be drawn in, to participate in the very evil Christians are so passionate to renounce. But Christians must not neglect their own pursuit of the very One they follow. Nor should they become detached from the encouragement, support, and accountability that only a local community of faith offers. After all, offering redemption and restoration is only possible when one is rooted.

For Jamie, restoration meant showing up at midnight in a stranger's drug-filled home. If you were to become a restorer, what would it look like? Who would you be provoked to help, heal, or love? Where would you show up that you don't currently frequent? Restoration really does start with a mind-set of response to the personal and cultural cues you are already receiving.

Let me offer a few specific observations on how a provoked Christian lives.

Engagement over Condemnation

Provoked Christians resist the urge to condemn everything that isn't explicitly Christian. They have a capacity to find goodness, truth, and beauty in most any creation.

I grew up in a conservative environment where the disapproval of culture was the norm. On Sunday afternoons, our living room was filled with the sound of football and NASCAR, but every time a beer commercial came on the television we had to turn the volume down. You might imagine how laborious this became for my brother and me during pre–remote control days, especially when watching sports, where every other commercial depicted beer as the constant companion for a great experience. The theory went: If we didn't hear the jingle, we'd be less likely to buy the lie. (Though maybe it worked, because I never became an alcoholic and still don't enjoy the taste of beer!)

Now, as a parent myself, I can see wisdom in this logic. Thanks to the DVR, I can fast-forward through commercials from the couch that aren't age-appropriate for my children. The bigger concern is how some Christians are taking this beyond responsible parenting. Many people train their children to avoid the "wrong" in culture, rather than model how to effectively engage and contribute to it. They still see mainstream culture as bad—and to be avoided at all costs.

Provoked Christians don't fear exposure to culture's ideas, products, and marketing campaigns; they learn to discern good from bad, truth from falsehood. Possessing discriminating taste, they eat and drink much of what the world has to offer. They appreciate opposing works by Richard Dawkins and opinionated rants by Christopher Hitchens without fear of being sucked into a wrong way of thinking. They work with people of different faiths to relieve social injustice in their communities. They are driven by the belief that Jesus himself was more concerned with engagement than condemnation. As John writes, "For God did not send his Son into the world to condemn the world, but to save the world through him" (Jn 3:17).

Grace over Judgment

Provoked Christians resist judging non-Christians.[6] Anecdotal research suggests that offended Christians have held those who never claimed to follow Jesus to a standard they haven't signed up for. They expect non-Christians to conform to the same moral code as a Christ follower. But does that set a realistic expectation?

Instead, the next Christians engage the world through a lens of grace.

When they encounter the Renees in their lives, they respond like Jamie did. He didn't place himself above her or consider himself better. He remembered that his path to following Jesus also involved a radical story of grace. He realized that everyone's journey looks different. This is a key lesson in learning to meet people wherever they are.

A mind-set of grace over judgment defines how restorers engage with all people. They don't exhibit this in word only—that's what judgment does. Instead, grace is active; it seeks out, responds, and loves deeply. The next Christians' "grace first" mentality allows them to get involved in the messy process of restoration with people and places most Christians normally avoid.

Courage over Comfort

A few years ago I met Gary Haugen, the founder of International Justice Mission (IJM), an organization that uses legal channels to fight injustices around the world, especially sex trafficking. Gary is a former investigator with the U.S. Department of Justice. He was sent to Rwanda in 1994 to investigate the genocide and identify the bodies of more than eight hundred thousand people massacred over ethnic strife. When he left Kigali to return home, something inside of him had morphed. He had never seen the results of injustice at this magnitude. Gary knew something must be done to combat the kind of horrific evil he had just witnessed. As a restoration-minded Christian would, he started IJM to be a part of the solution.

One summer morning, Gary and I met for breakfast at a café in Atlanta. He was unusually outspoken on a topic I had heard very few Christians address: the popular idea that Christians should pursue safety and comfort. Prior to the Rwanda assignment, he too was guilty of buying into the "safe Christian" premise, believing that his main duty was to protect his children from worldly corruption. For him, the Christian life was synonymous with the American dream: two cars and a suburban home in a gated community. But today, Gary's view is consistent with a provoked mind-set. He's no longer comfortable with just being comfortable.

Provoked Christians know that Christian faithfulness often means living dangerously on the front edges of pain in the world. Engaging the darkness takes courage and conviction. It requires a willingness to give up the pursuit of comfort. I often wonder, Who will have the courage to engage culture—which at times means confronting evil—if Christians won't?

Faithfulness over Reputation

When provoked, the next Christians engage the dirtiness of our world without fear of tarnishing their reputations. Their actions aren't affected by what others think. But I must offer a word of caution. When provoked Christians take up this challenge, they inevitably find themselves under scrutiny, often from those who love them most. Their concerned friends or family are perplexed that Christ would want someone in such places, hanging out with "those kind" of people.

Still, they follow the example of Jesus himself, who didn't have a glowing reputation among religious people. They place faithfulness to God above the potential that others will misunderstand their intentions. As Louie Giglio, founder of the Passion Movement, once told me, "At the end of your life, you will answer to God for what *he* has asked you to do in your life—not for what *others* wanted you to do."

Mike Foster demonstrates this kind of reputation abandonment more than anyone I know. Several years ago, he was overwhelmed with America's porn problem and decided to engage it. Most of the Christians around him were avoiding the conversation altogether, or simply taking a posture of condemnation. How else should good Christians respond to one of the most sordid aspects of our culture?

Mike thought differently. He saw an opportunity for restoration.

Mike recognized that the typical approach of creating content filters for online use was not working. He identified that the principal challenge in overcoming porn addiction was isolation and loneliness. Chronic masturbators were ashamed. Who would want to admit to fantasizing over pixels?

So his team created software called x3watch, which facilitates accountability between two people. When a user visits adult content sites, the software notifies his or her selected friend. This creates a conversation. Mike believed if people could talk about their porn addiction with someone they trust, it would go a long way toward healing and restoration. And it has.

Mike recognized something simple, yet profound: The people *making* pornography were just like him. They too were made in the image of God. Instead of categorizing them according to their sins and behavior, he viewed them with grace.

With his wife's support, Mike ventured out to the darkest of places—an adult entertainment expo. After creating an organization to befriend people inside the porn industry, he and his wife headed to Las Vegas to participate in the world's largest porn event. They listened, talked, and handed out free Bibles. The hot pink and yellow covers said it all: "Jesus Loves Porn Stars."

Since then, the organization has been to over twenty adult expos and has helped countless girls get out of an industry that is destined to destroy them. Even adult filmmakers have worked with him to expose and fight the injustices against women in the sex industry.

Many people have scrutinized Mike's approach, claiming he has gone too far, or that no Christians should place themselves in the middle of such wickedness. But Mike's testimony in this regard is impressive. He credits his daily time with God and his incredibly strong wife, Jen, for helping him stay grounded. He remains discerning and committed to those he knows God loves. He doesn't just show up at porn shows unprepared; he fasts, prays, and is very conscientious about controlling his exposure in the middle of that environment.

Mike's example is powerful and long overdue. One could easily argue that for too long Christians have avoided some of the raunchiest environments that were desperate for the light of God.

The sheer appearance of evil associated with pornography, drug addiction, alcohol, criminal activity, and many forms of music, film, and art are understandably offensive to some. The previous Christian approach would have been to boycott, condemn, and run away. For the next Christians, running away is not an option.

*   *   *

PERHAPS YOU'RE STILL not convinced that this expression of being Christian is biblical. Let me offer one more example from the apostle Paul and his encounter with the people of Athens (Acts 17:16–34). Here we find Paul confronted with the debauchery of a first-century global city. Luke describes Paul's reaction with great detail, saying that his "spirit was being provoked within him" (Acts 17:16, NASB) by the idolatry of the city. The biblical scholar John Stott explains the cultural setting: "Many of the idols and shrines were elegantly made by skilled artists, and filled Athens to the point that Xenophon spoke of the city as 'one great altar, one great sacrifice.' "[7] The historian E. M. Blaiklock even describes the stone pillars that adorned the city wall as "roughly fashioned with phallic attributes [that] stood as protecting talismans at every entrance in the city."[8] For most Christians today, the art, sculptures, and visual elements of the city would have been deeply offensive—the antithesis of sacred values.

Paul responds brilliantly.

He makes his way to the marketplace and synagogue to address their belief in idols. He shows up on their turf to have conversations about what it is he has observed. He recognizes that Athenians are pursuing something transcendent, albeit offensive. Paul is provoked to engage.

The Athenian philosophers invite him to their cultural nerve center—the Areopagus—where philosophers, musicians, artists, and innovators gathered to converse about their city's most pressing concerns. His message seems foreign to them. But now it was his turn to explain in their terms what he had been teaching.

Paul masterfully delivers what is now recognized as one of the most culturally engaging, yet spiritually informative speeches in the New Testament. He uses the setting he has observed—in particular, an idol named "unknown God"—to make his case to the intellectual leaders, judges, and philosophers of Athens. Paul explains that the "unknown God" to which they pray is representative of the one true God. He connects their search for God revealed in the artwork and statues of their city to the transcendent story of Jesus Christ.

Many rejected his reasoning, but others wanted to hear more. Some became Christians. Scripture mentions by name Dionysius, a judge of the Areopagus, and a woman named Damaris (Acts 17:34).

What Paul accomplished so intelligently gives us a model to follow. First, he recognized his role in the moment. He wasn't there to close the deal and lead everyone in the sinner's prayer, and he didn't condemn them all to hell for practicing idolatry, even though both of those responses held some merit. Instead, Paul trusted God's ability to fulfill his will in his own timing, and that freed Paul to exercise his unique ability to form an intellectual connection with the Athenians. They were deep thinkers, so Paul entered their world. As a result, they were enticed. They detected love, not rejection. They saw concern rather than judgment.

Paul validated their attempts to understand God, and he remembered how he himself once needed help to understand who Jesus was. He did not condemn them by preaching that they should tear down their idols. Instead, he presented his case with humility to reveal the truth of what it was they were really seeking—the hope of Christ.

Apart from Jesus, a better example hardly exists for the restoration-minded Christian than Paul's. Not only did he show up and engage—he showed compassion and grace to anyone who would listen. It appears his desire for people to be restored to Christ overcame any urges to be offended by their sin.

LIVING IN THE TENSION

I had just finished dinner when my phone rang. Jamie was animated; it had been a big week. After the five-day rehab three years ago when Renee ultimately experienced a full recovery, Jamie launched a nonprofit organization called To Write Love on Her Arms (TWLOHA). Built off the revenues of a simple T-shirt design by the same name, TWLOHA had really taken off. Because of the momentum, Hot Topic, the nation's number one hipster T-shirt company, decided to carry TWLOHA's trademark shirt. After one week on the shelf, the shirt became their best seller! Jamie was beside himself, humbled and excited that the message was breaking through in even the darkest of places.

Earlier that day, the owner of Hot Topic contacted Jamie with what seemed to be a major problem. They discovered the story of Renee's healing that was printed on the inside of every one of the shirts. In the story, Jamie recounts how his friends became Renee's "body of Christ." This mention of religion was a violation of company policy. How should Jamie respond? Be offended, or be provoked to engage?

It would have been easy to get upset at Hot Topic, or deride them for discrimination against religion. Some devout believers might have pulled the shirt from Hot Topic and staged a boycott of their products in order to stand up for Christ. On the other hand, Jamie could respect their policy and find a way to revise the story to contain no explicit religious references while still getting the message across.

Jamie made the decision to slightly modify the story. Understandably, some good Christians might take offense with this decision and question Jamie's capitulation, viewing it as weakness or even unjustifiable compromise. And maybe their concerns are valid. But like a true restorer, Jamie took the long view, choosing to still bring the redemptive power of Christ's love to an audience that's hardly ever exposed to it. As of this writing, it is still the biggest-selling T-shirt in Hot Topic stores across the country. Jamie's decision to respect the rules of this new pluralistic setting, while creatively expressing the story of God's love, has allowed the heart of the Gospel to bump into hundreds of thousands of young adults in unassuming ways.

As was the case with Jamie's story, the power of the Holy Spirit seems to work far better than our own vain attempts to "make it happen." Many times, the job of provoked Christians is to simply show up and let restoration thinking flood their actions and responses as they encounter a deeply broken world.

SIX

Creators, *Not Critics*

THE BOLD WORDS ACROSS THE MASTHEAD SAY IT WELL—
"Signs of Life in Music, Film and Culture." *Paste* magazine has
long been a cult favorite among talented and well-known musicians. *Rolling Stone* and *Spin* have nothing on it—artists claim
it's the best publication taking a deep, serious look at music and
film. Instead of filling its pages with celebrity gossip and political opinions, *Paste* focuses on highlighting the good, true, and
beautiful in culture.

Cofounders Nick Purdy and Josh Jackson describe their objective in creating *Paste* as simply a way to share with others the
music, films, books, and video games they love. They believe
that "pop culture isn't inert; it actually does something to you
as a person and affects your outlook on life and how you approach everything."[1] Their objective in creating *Paste* magazine
was to provide a filter for the "cultural air." They make it a bit
more breathable, not by censoring music with questionable lyrics or blackballing artists who at one point in their career have
done something shameful, but by highlighting themes and
thoughtful artistry portrayed in film and music. In doing so,
they affirm goodness that often goes overlooked.

Their approach seems to be working. Fans and industry

insiders alike have begun breathing this fresh air deeply. For the past three years, *Paste* has walked away with numerous industry awards and an exhaustive list of nominations for various design and excellence honors in their print and digital formats.[2] They have created something—a legitimate media company—that is not only valued by culture at large but is contributing to the restoration of God's goodness in society. Most important, they have experienced the power of creating a cultural good and seeing the impact it can have on millions of God's creations, Christian or not.

* * *

BY DEFINITION, WHEN we restore, we create something new that has a striking resemblance to the past. Rather than being stuck in the present, restorers run back to the other end of the timeline and focus on what once was—and what *should* be again. Then they create.

It's too easy to be drawn into an analysis of how bad things are when focused only on the present. *How did things get this way? Who's to blame? Why me?* The answers to these questions may be important, but only as a resource to inform the restoration. For example, a marksman doesn't hit the target by focusing on how *not* to miss it. He pours his time, energy, and resources into creating the perfect shot. In the process, the things that hinder his success fade to the periphery.

For the restorers I've gotten to know, this seems like their natural reflex. They respond to brokenness as if they see right through the moment and into a future that bears a mystical resemblance to the pristine state of the past. Then they work to create that future. Their unique vision enables them to face some of the greatest problems in our world without even a flinch.

Jamie Tworkowski did this well. For him, it was responding by not only helping Renee but also *creating* an awareness organization built around a simple T-shirt concept. As a result, a message of love, hope, and acceptance has reached an indigent population usually brushed to the fringes of society. Suicides have been prevented, rehabs are being funded, and a movement is under way—all because of one simple creation.

While creations like Jamie's To Write Love on Her Arms and Nick and Josh's *Paste* magazine are advancing great good in the world—affecting millions of people—they don't always lead to immediate conversions. And for these Christians, that's okay. They believe that part of service to God is bringing signs that point to his Kingdom and tangibly expressing his love to those in need—even when the measurable result of conversion can never be tallied.

Regardless of faith, class, or ethnicity—and no matter if they'll ever meet the recipients or not—these Christians feel bound to create goods that tell the truth about how the world works. They are using their talents to respond to the burdens God has placed within and in front of them. And the world is taking notice.

While being provoked is an important characteristic of restorers, no one solves anything from merely showing up. That is why the next Christians are provoked to *do* something when they arrive on the cultural scene—namely to create culture that can inspire change. They create organizations, services, and goods—art, films, music, campaigns, projects, media, churches, and businesses—anything that incarnates Christ and communicates the restoration that's possible. In this way, *creating* sits at the heart of restoration.

* * *

I USED TO think that for Christians to *really* do good, conversion of another person had to take place. But the next Christians have helped me think about this more deeply. They aren't just "do-gooders" who lack theological understanding. They believe that service to God reflects his Kingdom and tangibly expresses his love to those in need—even when conversions cannot be quantified. They see "doing good" as the perfect dance partner for conversion. Both are important, but neither one takes precedence over the other. Even the much-respected conservative evangelical theologian John Stott has affirmed that social action is a partner of evangelism: "As partners the two belong to each other and yet are independent of each other. Neither is a means to the other, or even a manifestation of the other. For each is an end in itself. Both are expressions of unfeigned love."[3]

The next Christians are living within the tension of both. They recognize from Scripture that faithfulness is displayed in both word *and* deed—seen best by combining the Great Commission's instruction to "make disciples" *with* the second greatest commandment to "love thy neighbor." The beauty of the Gospel is found in both proclamation *and* demonstration. Neither comes first; neither comes second. Like the perfect marriage, it's the duty of the Christian to take on each, giving 100 percent effort to both. As Paul reminds the church at Thessalonica, "Our gospel came to you not simply with words but also with power" (1 Thess 1:5). Rather than preaching a sermon and hoping people "got it," Christians were working miracles and doing good deeds among the people. They were true restorers.

These "common good" demonstrations of God's love are still valid and important today. These provoked next Christians know this and extend God's love to everyone, regardless of whether they are Christian or not, or ever become Christian or not.

Their way of living is rooted in Scripture and a little-understood historic Christian conception known as the *common good*. This simple phrase means "the most good for *all* people."[4] Aristotle first conceived it, but Thomas Aquinas, a thirteenth-century Roman Catholic philosopher, honed it well as a Christian conception for how Christians ought to live alongside others in society. This strict definition of the common good—the most good for all people—doesn't prefer one human being over another; instead, it values *all* human life and wants what is best for *all* people, Christian or not. It motivates these next Christians to care for *all* people, whether young, old, disabled, impaired, unborn, or otherwise different from themselves in race, religion, socioeconomic status, or worldview.

Practicing this common good mentality—where good deeds are also seen as integral to Christian mission—can actually have a positive impact on culture at large. When culture takes dark turns, Separatist Christians bemoan and lament society saying, "We did all we could do." But the efforts of these culture warriors and insiders, who have spent decades being critics of society, have been profoundly misguided. Andy Crouch, in his seminal book *Culture Making*, reminds us that these approaches aren't best. Cultures aren't changed by being condemned, critiqued, or copied. He concludes, "The only way to change culture is to *create* more of it."[5]

From magazines like *Paste* to nonprofit organizations, environmental policy, documentaries, educational institutions, and awareness campaigns, all the way to the goods and services shaped within their own workplace, the next Christians are fast at work creating good culture. In doing so, they aren't just reconstructing what's broken; they are adding on a new dimension in the places they've been called to—restoring the truth, goodness, and beauty that's been lost.

CREATING CULTURE

You might be thinking that creating culture sounds lofty, sophisticated, and almost off-putting. If you are picturing grandiose visions that require an artistic wiring, tons of money, or an influential media outlet, you may be missing the point. It is less theoretical than it sounds. Let me start by describing what culture is and then examine how these Christians are creating it.

As Nick and Josh said, "Culture is the air you breathe."[6] It's all around you: the clothes you wear, the music you listen to, the books you read, the car you drive, the organization you receive your paycheck from, and the school your children attend. From shoes and barbecue chicken pizza to churches and civic organizations, each creation, or "good," represents a cultural artifact made by someone at some point in time. Now, some of these may seem like small creations compared to the Red Cross, Harvard University, or the hydrogen fuel cell. But the reality is that the cultural goods we use or encounter play a role in our everyday life experiences. They are seeping into our bloodstream whether we realize it or not.

Additionally, each cultural artifact tells a story about the inventor's view of the world. Consider the last movie you enjoyed. What story did the movie tell about the world? Did the plotline affirm authentic relationships *or* celebrate their demise? Did the main character illustrate the pain and loss of trust when one spouse cheats on the other *or* did it glorify the

fleeting emotional high of a promiscuous rendezvous? Reflecting on these kinds of questions tells us whether a film reveals
the truth or a lie about reality. Or, take a more obvious example. Does the china cabinet in your house tell a story of craftsmanship and beauty *or* of speed and mass production? If it's
coated in a "faux-wood" veneer, it tells the story of the latter.[7]
Whether films or furniture, the kinds of goods we create say a
lot about their creator and how things ought to be. And the
next Christians recognize that.

They see in God's original job description for mankind that
they have a role in partnering with God to fill the earth—*creating culture* that affirms his values of goodness, truth, and beauty.
This shouldn't surprise us that being "creators" is embedded in
our original human DNA. We are all made in the image of our
Creator and he has called us to exercise our dominion and
stewardship by creating and cultivating culture on earth (Gn
1–2). Though sin corrupts our world, desires, and motivations,
we can continue to partner with God as culture creators to restore his intentions for our world.

Based on a common good mentality, these Christians aren't
confounded by only thinking about how to get people "saved."
They have freed their minds to dream about how they can serve
in God's Kingdom. Here are a few ways the next Christians are
creating culture.

Culture That Celebrates Beauty

Nikolle Reyes and her husband, José, are intrigued by the
beauty of classical music. They enjoy the art form and interplay
between composer and musician while appreciating the tech-
nical difficulty of mastering an instrument. The mystery of

why well-performed chamber music could arouse hidden parts of their soul has always fascinated them. It has made them long to experience that sensation more. Inviting their twenty-something friends to the stodgy, highbrow, prestigious auditoriums that exclusively house this style of music was not going to work.

After a few lunchtime discussions with their friend Fia Durrett, who is a professional violinist, they decided to *do something.* In 2007, the Reyeses and the Durretts partnered to create Fringe, a cultural good for the community of Atlanta to enjoy. Fringe was slated to be an entirely new experience in the arts that blended film, chamber music, and visual art. Their vision was to give people a fuller, more infectious experience with beauty and the arts—and they delivered.

Opening night was standing room only: They packed the two-hundred-seat auditorium provided by their church. Participants enjoyed short films and a DJ spinning ambient electronica between concertos by Brahms and Kodály! Wearing jeans and mingling comfortably among a local painter's displayed art, a new generation was being reintroduced to a blend of music and art in a forum they could appreciate. Writing for the *Atlanta Journal Constitution,* Pierre Ruhe described their creative innovation as the perfect synthesis "combining what's normal inside a concert hall (performances of the old classics) with what's normal in the rest of society (the TV-driven media culture)."[8]

So how does something like Fringe promote God's Kingdom? Shouldn't there be a subliminal statement of belief, an invitation to a local church, or a logo for a ministry in there somewhere?

When the next Christians create culture that promotes

beauty, they give people a glimpse of the beauty of God. There's no need for a logo, because the beauty itself belongs to God and is a pronouncement for his existence, love, and desire for the world. It happens so quickly but leaves us with a thirst for more—like the power of a fading sunset or the glory of a duck landing on a pond. These moments point people toward God because "beauty is *both* something that calls us out of ourselves *and* something which appeals to feelings deep within us."[9] It's most obvious in nature as well as the cultural goods we create.

Inviting fellow human beings to experience beauty teases their souls and allows them, albeit briefly, to see a picture of how things ought to be.

Culture That Affirms Goodness

All of us bear the image of God and, with it, the ability to create goods and environments that affirm goodness. Let me explain by telling you a bit about a few of my neighbors.

Chris and Diana are the consummate hosts, always creating a place for families to spend time together. Their home is filled with the laughter of children—and even adults—especially during college football season. They've *created* an environment where human relationships and community flourish. I imagine it's just the way God intended friendships to be.

Consider Jim's hankering for order, safety, and perfection. As a transportation engineer, he ensures that on- and off-ramps and bridge overpasses are perfectly designed to be safe, efficient, and helpful. He is actively creating a cultural good—a highway system—from which everyone else benefits. His specialized attention to detail reflects God's own caring attention for design.

Josephine volunteers at our local school working with children in the special needs program. She has a heart full of compassion and affirms goodness by helping children build off of their potential. She sees the best in them and helps them achieve it.

I think about my neighbor Dennis and his uncanny ability to repeatedly win "Yard of the Month." Sure, he's got a great green thumb, but it's just one more indication of his appreciation for craftsmanship. He admires good work and using his own hands to *create*. From finishing his own basement to carefully manicuring his emerald green lawn, Dennis affirms beauty and goodness through his creations.

Sometimes we must create culture in seemingly bankrupt places. Mike Foster affirmed the talent of a porn director by hiring him to help create a public service message about the negative effects of pornography. Such a choice seems ironic, but that was the point. Mike wanted to recruit the porn director to help him make a major statement about what's wrong with porn! Together, they created a good in the form of an awareness campaign. Whatever the case may be, Christ wants us to have eyes to see goodness wherever it shows up. When goodness is revealed, the world gets one more opportunity to catch a glimpse of God's restoration work in progress.

For the next Christians, this perspective allows them to see the work of the divine emanating from everyone. When they see it, they call it out, celebrate it, and affirm its *goodness*. They embody the words of the Apostle Paul: "Whatever you do, whether in word or deed, do it all in the name of the Lord Jesus" (Col 3:17).

Culture That Tells the Truth

William Wilberforce led the Clapham Circle—an informal collective of British legislators, artists, and business and religious leaders—who confronted the slave economy in the late 1700s, ultimately leading to its collapse. At the time, people assumed that black people were inferior to other human beings. The thought of eliminating slavery threatened the ruling class's power and society's very existence. Abolition was an incredibly dangerous and bold idea to pursue. Wilberforce understood that changing the attitudes of his society and creating a new culture that affirmed the dignity of all humans would require more than just eloquent speeches. He needed a cultural good that could spread the message farther than just the steps of Parliament. So the Clapham Circle decided to get busy creating.

He and his fellow abolitionists proclaimed the truth about slavery in a way that compelled people. They approached Josiah Wedgwood, the queen's potter, and persuaded him to create a special cameo for their cause. In the cameo was a silhouette of a slave kneeling in shackles with the inscription: "Am I Not a Man and a Brother?" People began to wear this cameo on their outer coats and reproduce it on everything from plates to snuffboxes. Even women, who at the time could not vote, would proudly wear them to show their support for abolition.[10] This cultural good told the truth about slavery by confronting people with a simple question. But it also had the coalition-building effect of getting the masses involved in one of the most important justice issues of the day—all because of a little one-by-two-inch piece of clay ingeniously prescribed for their moment (and you thought LIVESTRONG bracelets were a novel idea).

In the same way, the next Christians create goods that tell the truth about the world. They paint pictures of how the world ought to be. For a talented artist like Jeremy Cowart, it means telling the truth through his photography. In his visual book *Hope in the Dark,* his photographs juxtapose the brokenness of an AIDS-stricken mom (truth about corruption) with the hope of a child drinking clean water for the first time (how things ought to be).[11]

While some of the examples I've given require artistic ability or an entrepreneurial spirit, anyone can create redemptive culture. For a working mom, it may mean organizing a company-wide charity fund-raiser that addresses a pressing need in her community. Creating culture doesn't always mean new invention. More likely, it will be a natural by-product of talents you have already applied in the places you already frequent. Creating culture isn't only about making movies, writing about art, or starting movements. If you are an image-bearer—and we all are—then you *can* create.

Culture That Serves

Some Christians are creating and cultivating good culture simply by serving others in their neighborhoods, on their campuses, and throughout cities. As human beings, and especially as Christians, we have a special calling to address the basic needs of others. Part of our responsibility is "to feed, to clothe, and to protect"—which cultivates the common basis for how life is structured in a pluralistic society.[12]

In metropolitan Atlanta, Christian leaders Chip Sweeney, Norwood Davis, Bryan Crute, and Crawford Loritts oversee a collective of churches called Unite! They've dedicated their energy to facilitate partnerships with dozens of churches that help thousands of volunteers take on restoration projects that improve the lives of those in their city. From painting schools to volunteering at local food pantries, these Christians show their concern for the city by being involved in it. What began with just one weekend of service has now motivated a year-round commitment to justice, education, family, and reducing poverty. Their projects aren't particularly original or ingenious—but they have created a unifying idea that helps people serve.

Being creators is one way these Christians are confronting corruption and advancing the common good for *all* people. As Tim Keller writes, Christians are "called not just to live in the city, but also to love it and work for its *shalom*—its economic, social, and spiritual flourishing. . . . The citizens of God's city are the best possible citizens of their earthly cities."[13]

But there's a counterfeit idea that I call the *predominant good.* And there's very little good about it. Predominant good is based on the idea of the collective public interest. It's a different take on the common good but with a glaring distinction worth noting. The definition of the *public interest* is "the most good for the *most* people." Notice the one word change—instead of good for "all" people, it's only for "most" people. By default, this counterfeit idea makes room to exclude those who have nothing helpful to offer to the "most." Taking this view to its logical extreme, the strongest survive and the weak are left to fend for themselves. The majority (or, more often, those in power) does what's best for itself and protects its way of life, devaluing those with little voice in the system—the disabled, the elderly, the poor, the unborn, or anyone who could threaten the money, time, and resources of the majority.

Predominant good may sound similar to the common good, but it is deeply unchristian. It's the opposite of restoration and runs counter to the way Jesus valued *all* people. In his parable of the lost sheep, Christ takes great care to pursue and find the one sheep that was lost. He left the other ninety-nine, because one had gotten separated from the flock. He didn't do the "most good for the most sheep" as the collective public interest would deem good. Had he done that, he would have stayed with the ninety-nine and left the one to fend for himself. Instead, Jesus leaves the ninety-nine in pursuit of the one. In God's equation, everyone matters—and that undergirds the next Christians' mentality to create goods with the potential to touch all people.

Common ground thinking is revolutionizing activities among present-day Christians. Entire churches finally feel free to serve their communities and the world using all their talents. Churches are beginning to feel the power of seeing all their congregants come alive, from doctors co-opting to create clinics for the poor in urban centers to stay-at-home moms starting afterschool tutoring programs for at-risk children. They'd bought in to the modern idea that the only good Christian activity was to convert others or give their money and time to those who could. Today they are discovering that their talent and creativity matter. The longings they have felt to do good in the world—even if it wasn't explicitly connected to getting people saved—have been validated. And they are thrilled to give their time, energy, money, and life to creating and cultivating culture in a way that allows God's love to break through on earth today.

* * *

I'll never forget the moment Rebekah and I welcomed our firstborn son into the world. It was quite a day. A routine ob-gyn appointment turned into an emergency C-section for the delivery. Once born, Cade was immediately placed into intensive care—Rebekah never even had the opportunity to hold him. As rookies, we were already nervous about the new challenges parenthood would bring, but this was pushing us to our limits. Around two o'clock the next morning, a doctor barged into our room, abruptly waking us. I was still in a slumber and completely unemotional when he stumbled to deliver the news: "We think your son has Down syndrome. We'll send off the blood tests tomorrow to confirm." Our hearts sank.

We were in emotional shock and somewhat despondent. We held each other, exhausted after a long, long day, quietly trying to reassure ourselves that everything would be okay. But even though we didn't voice it, we couldn't help but feel a sense of sadness and fear about the future. Our lives had just taken a dramatic turn, and we weren't sure how we'd respond.

Cade's diagnosis was only the beginning.

Since those days nine years ago, our journey has been great. Sure, we've had our share of challenges—the typical ups and downs of any new parent—but we've grown up. Cade has taught us so much about life and love. His smile and delight bring a warmth to our world we never knew could exist. He's taught us to appreciate the simple things in life—and to laugh hard at some of the silliest!

Our eyes have been opened. We have been startled to realize that Cade is a Down syndrome survivor. I'm sure that may sound odd and a bit dramatic, but, bear with me, it's not.

Very few Down syndrome babies make it into this world.[14] Many pregnant and expectant parents who are presented with a prenatal diagnosis of Down syndrome are faced with a serious life-or-death decision. And when presented with this dilemma, an overwhelming majority chooses to terminate the life of their baby. They believe this is best—that they are sparing themselves and their future child from what appears to be a difficult future for the entire family.

As you might expect, over the years Rebekah and I have become good friends with other parents in a similar situation. One of the consistent story lines we've heard over and over is how much pressure these mothers felt to terminate their pregnancies once prenatal testing showed the possibility of a Down syndrome diagnosis. To our surprise, they weren't alone— research backs up their feelings.

When given a prenatal diagnosis of Down syndrome, 90 percent of mothers choose to terminate their babies.[15] Ninety percent! No matter where you come down on the abortion issue, that number is staggering. Unfortunately, when parents are faced with this diagnosis, everything in the culture points them toward the baby's extinction. Insurance companies don't want to pay the long-term health care bills, the government isn't eager to carry the weight of future expenses, and doctors want to avoid malpractice suits at all costs. The fear of the unknown for shocked parents usually leads to a decision to abort; even when up to 5 percent of these diagnoses are false positives.[16]

Rebekah and I were compelled to get involved. We wanted to do something to advocate for these precious children. The question became: How should we engage this issue? We could have gotten involved the way we'd seen many other Christians engage the abortion issue: by calling it out as murder, joining pro-life protests, helping to elect pro-life candidates, and even carrying the fight to the abortion clinics themselves. Or, we could look for a more solution-oriented way to approach this issue. What if we could create something that could possibly reduce the rate to 80, 70, or even 50 percent in the years ahead? Protest has been the modus operandi for many Christians over the past several decades and has yielded little progress. Our approach seemed fresh and had the potential to accomplish a lot of good in our world today.

For those around us, it seemed ambitious if not crazy to take on such a big issue. Working together with our friends Justin and Stephanie and a local advocacy association, we created a booklet called *Understanding a Down Syndrome Diagnosis.* Committed parents distributed the booklets to every ob-gyn's and geneticist's office in metro Atlanta. The booklet attempted to succinctly address the specific concerns of parents-to-be, summarized the latest scientific discoveries, and pointed them to the resources most helpful at the point of receiving the diagnosis. It also included beautiful photographs that captured the extraordinary and quite normal lives individuals with Down syndrome lead. And the campaign provided business cards with the contact information of experienced parents who were available for counsel and support. Doctors committed to be more thoughtful in how they delivered the diagnosis and to offer these booklets as part of the process. We hoped this cultural good could aid in restoring dignity to the lives of these precious children by affirming their goodness and telling the truth.

Producing the booklet was a small act in the big scheme of things. It's impossible to track its total effectiveness, but I am confident that forging new ground in this way was the right thing to do. Today other city associations are starting to use these materials to spread the word in their communities. If telling the truth more creatively helps just one more child enter this world full of possibilities, it was definitely worth it.

Creating instead of criticizing takes discipline. And the cost of inaction, laziness, and fear is undoubtedly high. When we don't respond, needs go unmet and we miss out on what God wants to do through us and, just as important, *in us*. But it's not easy. For the Christian who wants to participate in God's restoration project it will mean taking risks. If you don't, the world might just miss out on an opportunity to experience God's goodness through you.

I've met so many people with unrealized creative ideas that could solve problems in our world. Talk is cheap, and the next Christians realize that putting their money where their heart is and giving extra time and energy to pursue the cravings God has placed inside of them will yield exponential change. The irony about culture is that you can never predict what creation just might affect the world. Ultimately, that is not for us to decide. It's our job to be faithful to respond to the brokenness of culture with an eye for the Creator's original intent. That perspective enables us to create new cultural goods that reflect God's own essence by celebrating beauty, affirming goodness, telling the truth, and serving the needs of others. With those responsibilities fulfilled, we are free to let God take care of the rest.

SEVEN

Called, *Not Employed*

THE FINGERPRINTS OF INDUSTRIALIZATION CAN BE SEEN ALL over modern-day Christianity. In particular, the specialization of labor—a concept designed to engender speed and progress—is reflected in our Christian tradition of carefully distinguishing the "ministry" category from all others. We educate, train, and hire "professional ministers," placing a higher spiritual value on certain jobs and professions (like direct evangelism and service) and marking others (such as entertainment, academia, and science) as off-limits to orthodox Christians.

There are many practical benefits to this approach, but there are complications as well. For example, everyday Christians can develop an overdependence on formal ministry organizations. What's more, they are conditioned to view their own jobs as separate from "real ministry."

This is a shame, because we spend most of our waking hours in the workplace. Work provides the only real contact many Christians have with outsiders. For some it becomes their platform to evangelize by hosting Bible studies over lunch or awkwardly inserting prayer into places it doesn't seem to fit. For other conventional Christians, work has little or no connection to their faith. The spiritual value of their work is purely instrumental. Work is a place they can earn extra income to be handed over to the church for more obvious "spiritual" missions. As columnist David Brooks observes, "Evangelical Christians are practically absent from entire professions, such as academia, the media and filmmaking."[1]

However, the next Christians are reconsidering their vocations. They reject the false distinctions that have caused ideological polarization—not dissimilar to the left versus right politics on cable news—between the religious and secular parts of society. The next Christians see this polarization as having arbitrarily alienated millions from the Gospel and have chosen to counter it by reintegrating the good news into areas of society that the church had given up on in their parents' generation.

* * *

OWEN LEIMBACH IS a renaissance man to all who know him. He lives with his wife and three boys in Venice Beach, an eclectic neighborhood in Southern California. This thirty-four-year-old is the most unusually tall techno-political skateboarder you'll ever meet. Don't get me wrong, he can dress it up for executive meetings, but he prefers wearing jeans, T-shirts, and Vans and skating to work most mornings. At six feet four, he's quite a sight landing ollies on the sidewalk—it's just his style. He's quirky, hard to pin down, and, as you'd expect, steeped in the local SoCal vernacular—he uses phrases like "OG" (original gangster) and "hombre" to give his best compliments to those he respects.

Upon deeper inspection, Owen is the antislacker. His gifts in problem solving and online technology have helped him advance many career successes. He launched one of the first online colleges in the country and helped the White House create the world's largest volunteer matching system. Owen's résumé speaks for itself.

In 2003, Owen worked at ground zero for youth culture, music, and entertainment—a little outfit called MTV. Since its inception, Christian groups have criticized MTV and all of its progeny. With its promotion of artists, music, and programming that often ran roughshod over Christian sensibilities, it was an easy target for the faithful. Crawling in bed with MTV meant social death for any "legitimate" Christian.

Perceptions didn't stop Owen. He seized the opportunity to work at the media giant, viewing it as a long-overlooked channel to participate in a larger conversation that was shaping a generation.

His first assignment at MTV was producing the online coverage of the 2004 presidential election. That year the network— famous for doing "boxers or briefs" lovefests with Democratic candidates during election years—broadened their coverage to include all major parties, candidates, and issues.

Owen found a small but dedicated group at MTV who believed the network should use its "superpowers for good." Following the unanticipated success of the 2004 election coverage, they launched a permanent department charged with galvanizing youth to get involved in their communities and take responsibility for their actions. "Think MTV" was born. Owen and the religious pariah began engaging young adults on issues like faith, the environment, war, and peace.

Like Owen, the next Christians view every corner of society as "in play." They may not overtly use their platforms to evangelize, but the redemptive elements of their work are unmistakable. They've checked their moralizing stick at the door, but embrace the opportunity to naturally infuse faith into their businesses. If the conversations arise, they are thrilled to have them, but that isn't the only way they can be faithful. They understand that where they work is oftentimes the place God has called them to let his restoration flood the world. And who could argue with that?

The next Christians don't work at jobs; they serve in vocations. They see their occupational placement as part of God's greater mission. This view is natural and holistic, and fits within the everyday rhythms of most people's lives. Most of the time, the ideal space to begin "creating" is the one you already inhabit.

Remember when Jesus ate dinner with Zacchaeus? Jesus didn't tell Zacchaeus to quit his job. Instead, he inspired the tax collector to change the way he did his work: to be honest, not take advantage of people, and return fourfold what had been taken (Lk 19). When Jesus miraculously healed people, he didn't ask them to leave their towns and villages to follow him: He told them to go back to their normal way of life in celebration of a God who had intervened in their affairs (Mk 5). Often, when Jesus encountered others, they were transformed but not uprooted.

In this same way, the next Christians are staying put. Being a pastor, serving on a local church staff, or doing full-time missions work is no longer a prerequisite for doing ministry. While some may be called to full-time religious work, they accept that many Christians should simply work to restore the needs right under their noses. They've grown tired of being regarded as second-class Christians and want to be empowered on mission right where they are.[2] They see the need all around them for Christians to show up and restore in their neighborhoods and workplaces. They don't have to look far. The needs are obvious: If they don't fill the gap, who will? They understand the Gospel and know that God's desire for restoration applies to every corner of the world, including theirs.

THE SEVEN CHANNELS OF CULTURAL INFLUENCE

As we learned in chapter 6, culture isn't just a concept. Millions of goods, services, organizations, history, and attitudes pervade our way of life and make up a culture. Everyone plays some role in it—big or small—including you. Seeing it this way helps culture become less nebulous and more tangible. And in a similar way, the method by which we come into contact with the ideas culture distributes is just as real.

Several friends understood this principle well when they first convened in Warrenton, Virginia, back in 1988. This gathering of 175 leaders representative of various cultural institutions, who came together around an important set of issues, was monumental. They believed their ideas could have consequences if they were smart and tactical and could keep their message simple.[3]

But as an underwhelming minority, the odds were stacked against them to truly effect change. They came together from every corner of society, setting aside their personal agendas and differences to unite around the central tenets of a movement. They determined to advance their cause strategically and tactically one step at a time. And advance they did.

These friends formed the beginnings of what is now known as the gay movement. Hold on. I'm not saying this movement is an example of Christian restoration, but there are some lessons to be learned from their achievements. Ironically, the group that began the gay movement followed some profound cultural dynamics. In the process, they showed us what it looks like to work the levers of cultural influence with mastery.

Their accomplishments inform us. Those committed activists worked alongside average Americans to help a faction find its stride in American culture by the mid-1990s. They demonstrated the power of showing up right where they worked and letting their ideology and beliefs permeate everything they did.

Here's how it worked.

Their movement systematically inundated every sphere of society with the message of civility, tolerance, and equal rights for gays. As Paul Rondeau points out in "Selling Homosexuality to America," "their strategy was employed in five important markets of social influence . . . which touch every citizen in America: government, education, organized religion, the media, and the workplace."[4] In the business channel, vigorous attempts for same-sex couples to be recognized with benefits equal to those of married couples were finally successful.[5] In the education channel, books like *Heather Has Two Mommies* and *Daddy's Roommate* about same-sex parenting found their way into schools and public libraries. On television, *Ellen, Will and Grace,* and *Queer Eye for the Straight Guy* recast the image of gays and lesbians as fun, engaging, and talented trendsetters. Within the cultural channel of the church, major denominations like the Episcopal Church and the United Church of Christ opened leadership roles for gays and lesbians.[6] No corner of society would go untouched.

I'm not suggesting we celebrate the rise of the gay movement. Perhaps you're offended that I've even used it as an illustration. Instead of taking offense, be provoked! Their ability to shift cultural thought highlights a sociological principle that has been at work for centuries: When leaders disperse through-out all spheres of society—or "channels of culture"—and work together toward a common goal, change can happen.

With a few exceptions, cultural anthropologists generally agree that there are several cultural tentacles that reach every person. I've designated seven "channels of cultural influence," because they represent the institutions and industries that are consistently shaping culture.

Most people fit into one or more of these channels. Those who aren't directly contributing to a particular one are likely influenced by it. For instance, even if you don't work in the film industry, the latest movie you saw probably affected your atti-tude and imagination. You may not be a politician, but the laws they make have a profound impact on your life, and so on.

The spread of ideas—specifically, the Christian idea of restoration—will happen best and most powerfully when every channel of culture is leveraged. Keeping restoration isolated just to the church channel will only further separate Christians from the rest of the world. It's one explanation given for why parts of our culture have grown darker in recent decades. Christians separated and retreated, leaving a vacuum where others have spread their ideas instead. We left our posts.

Consider the gay movement again. Their success at spread-ing an idea through all seven channels of culture was obvious. In just thirty years, the idea of being gay has moved from being abnormal and abhorrent in society to being an acceptable and normal alternative lifestyle. This change of perception didn't just happen—it came about as a result of leaders embodying their ideology and message wherever they showed up each day.

As a natural by-product of God's plan for his Kingdom, the next Christians are being dispersed as restorers throughout all

SEVEN CHANNELS OF
CULTURAL INFLUENCE

MEDIA

Television
Radio
Publishing
Newspapers
Internet

EDUCATION

Public Schools
Private Schools
Charter Schools
Home School
College + University + Graduate
Adult + Continuing Ed

ARTS & ENTERTAINMENT

Artists
Film
Literature
Music
Fine Art + Performing Arts
Sports
Theater
Video Game Entertainment

BUSINESS

Advertising + Marketing + Public Relations
E-commerce + Retailers + Services
Finance + Investments + Securities
Legal

Technology + Biotech + Nanotech
Science + Medicine

GOVERNMENT

Executive
Judicial
Legislative
Military
Public Policy + Advocacy Groups

SOCIAL SECTOR

Educational
Family
Foundations + Trusts
Marriage
Religious

CHURCH

Local Churches
Para-Church Organizations

channels of culture. They are carrying the message of Jesus—bringing restoration, renewal, and healing; fighting injustice; telling the truth; affirming goodness; and celebrating beauty—in their places of service. They play a key role in overcoming the evil that otherwise overwhelms everything.[7]

From genetic scientists to artists, businesspeople to educators, these Christians are letting their gifts flood the world from the place they feel called to work. They don't only serve the need of the moment, but bring a bigger, overarching viewpoint to their fields. They have a keen eye to sense what is missing, broken, or corrupted and are courageous enough to respond. Put simply, the next Christians recognize their responsibility "not only to build up the church but also to build a society to the glory of God."[8]

Brokenness exists within each channel of culture. Our role isn't merely to run reports, create spreadsheets, and show up on time. We are called to find the things that are broken and affect them in some positive way. This is where calling begins to play itself out in every realm of our world, from media centers like MTV to entire public education systems.

RESTORING IN EVERY CHANNEL OF CULTURE

Sajan George, a respected pioneer in the education channel, unexpectedly found himself standing in the minefield of local politics. His role as a partner with Alvarez & Marsal is to develop turnaround strategies for underperforming organizations. He and his team determine the flaws within failing business models and restructure them for success.

In 2006, New York mayor Michael Bloomberg and Chancellor

Joel Klein asked Sajan and his team to help "turn around" the chronically underperforming New York City school system. They had observed the work of Sajan and his team's work with other local governments, and felt a partnership might help fix the broken, $14 billion system. Sajan sensed an opportunity for restoration.

He and his team got to know the system and went to work. Under Bloomberg and Klein's leadership, they moved the financial control from bureaucratic officials into the hands of the school principals on the ground. They reversed the inequity that had driven the previous system to the brink. By reorienting the funding mechanisms, schools in poor neighborhoods would now be able to control their own destinies—ensuring the "good schools" didn't just exist in the "good neighborhoods." Principals voluntarily signed on to be accountable for the learning of the children in their care. In a short time, the system was experiencing transformation.

Sajan's team saved the city $290 million—real money that could be reallocated back into the classroom. Everyone was thrilled with the restoration of a more *just* school system. In 2007, the New York City public schools received the coveted Broad Prize for the nation's most improved urban public school system. This engagement was a smashing success.

Working in the education channel as a Christian, Sajan had taken his responsibility to restore culture seriously. Fixing broken school systems wasn't in his original company charter, but it was a chance to promote justice, help children, and repair something that had been corrupted. And this opportunity showed up in the place he worked every day.

* * *

Dan Cooper is an investment portfolio manager working in the business channel. His Chicago-based company decided to change the game by taking a completely different angle on how business was evaluated. They recognized that the market typically didn't factor in character or integrity when forecasting the success of companies on the New York Stock Exchange. So with a private investor, they created a fund themselves to begin tracking the character, integrity, and overall quality of CEOs. Dan asked over three hundred Wall Street analysts a series of questions no one had ever posed to them before, such as "Which of the companies and CEOs that you follow would put the company before their own personal interest?"

By applying this new character matrix to more than three thousand CEOs running the world's largest companies, they began to place their bets on over one hundred companies that were led by CEOs with high integrity and character. As a result, their portfolio has consistently outperformed the market by 7 percent year over year since inception.

Their innovation provided a new way for money managers to consider where to invest. This cultural good created in Dan's channel of influence affirmed character over greed, and inspired more of what's truly good for people and industries alike. Today, the fund offers a new way for the investment community to consider how it allocates capital. Dan proved that these qualitative values aren't inconsequential—they matter.

* * *

Jon Passavant is one of the most successful male models in the fashion industry, but he's also a restorer. You might be asking, How can someone whose job is to "look good" work to restore creation in his current occupation? But Jon is more than an attractive face.

His work takes him all over the world, exposing him to a wide array of cultural channels affected by fashion brands and advertising. After Hurricane Katrina devastated the Gulf Coast, Jon and his agent developed a plan to play a role in restoring New Orleans. They decided to recruit the top male models in the industry to head to Louisiana and serve for a week with Habitat for Humanity. After months of planning, twenty-five models, a few photographers, and several major fashion companies landed in the heart of the ravaged bayou to begin construction on a new home. They called their work the Model Home Project.

* * *

THESE EXAMPLES LEAD to one of the most interesting opportunities before the American church today. The next Christians are already planted deep within each of these seven channels of culture where they are applying a restoration mind-set to the situations they encounter. Indeed, they are already positioned to affect the cultural landscape in a big way, just by virtue of how they interact in their vocations. And this presents a dramatic paradigm shift.

The churches that recognize that this move is under way find themselves in the middle of what could be the greatest transformation in how Christians have consistently engaged culture in a century. It has all the signs of being a manifestation as crucial as the Reformation was.

It's important to see the tension and what seems to be breaking through on the horizon. For decades, many Christians have thought the only place they could impact the Kingdom was through serving in their local churches. The church was the sole place they could express their gifts, whether volunteering or giving to local or international missions work. But the faithful are coming alive as a new generation of Christians are making the real connections between their faith and their work.

The church remains the epicenter of what is possible. It's the most uniquely positioned channel of cultural influence when it's operating on all cylinders. No other institution regularly convenes people who work within the other six channels of culture on a weekly basis. On any given Sunday in the church, leaders from all seven channels join together to pray, worship, learn, and socialize in one place. Then they are sent out, dispersed to support one another and to work within the sphere of society God has gifted and called them to in order to carry out his restoration work.

Imagine what is possible when Christians throughout the church recover this sense of vision for their work in the world. It could change everything about the movement of Jesus.

FINDING YOUR CALLING

What does that mean for *you* specifically? What might *your calling* be in the world today? It's a big question with no easy, prepackaged answers. In fact, each person's role is unique. But there are a few themes I've observed in the next Christians that make understanding *calling* more accessible.

Scott Harrison grew up in a church where he played keyboard for the worship team. He was very involved and incredibly dedicated to the church. Although faith had always been a huge part of Scott's life, he had grown tired of all the rules that came with it. He knew he was made for something more—something big—but didn't know how he'd discover it. At the age of eighteen, he decided to explore true meaning for himself in the context of nightlife entertainment in the Big Apple.

By the time he had turned twenty-three, his years of work had paid off. He was producing shows, calling the shots, and setting the rules. The only way you got into his clubs was to buy bottles of high-end vodka ($300 each) or be the best-dressed girl on the velvet rope. But this decadent life was taking its toll. A few years later, at the age of twenty-eight, while on "the perfect vacation" in Mexico surrounded by women, drugs, alcohol, and servants meeting his every need, he felt completely empty. That's when God began to work.

Scott began to see clearly the man he had become. He sat on the beach reading A. W. Tozer's *Pursuit of God* and started to feel his heart being restored. He wrestled with what he spent his days and nights working on. The question of calling kept coming up as he sensed God had something more meaningful for him to do with his talents. But he didn't know what.

Scott left his vacation and flew back to New York a changed person. When he arrived back home he was focused on a singular objective—transforming his current life into one that allowed him to serve God with his talent and passion. He had no idea what that would mean, but he was committed to doing whatever was necessary to figure it out.

Scott's dilemma was nothing new. Most people are seeking the age-old answer to the question Rick Warren made famous: "What on earth am I here for?"[9] People are longing for connection to a deeper purpose but struggle to find it. Beleaguered by too many options, we flip-flop on everything. Whether selecting a college major, or changing jobs every few years, or relocating from city to city, or trying to find a place to call home, many people are feeling more empty. Their search for significance ends each day at a bar, or alone in their bed, when all they really wanted was to find someone to listen and help them figure life out. They wake up just as alone the next morning, feeling discouraged, no closer to finding the magic answer and weary of living the rat race. On occasion, they spot someone who seems to have it all figured out, and it makes them utterly jealous. Deep down, they want someone else's story to be their story. They just feel stuck.

This is the story line for many young Americans, and it's no different for Christians. God created each of us for a unique purpose, but most people never invest the time and energy to discover it. When they do, many are scared away by the changes a new direction might bring. But sometimes the issue isn't a lack of courage; it's a lack of clarity. Amid all the options, we just don't know how to discern what it is we are supposed to do.

TALENTS, BURDENS, AND PURPOSE

A few years ago, I flew out to Boulder, Colorado, to spend some time with Pete Richardson. He's a counselor, a life coach, and a trusted friend. Pete is about fifteen years my elder and a real fatherly type—always offering encouragement and just the right word when I need it. He possesses the kind of wisdom and insight that only a life of rich experience and reflection can bring. He has a knack for helping leaders find their unique role in life and to discover their calling. There isn't a friend who was struggling with these significant questions who I wouldn't send to Pete—I know, because he has helped many of them resolve these kinds of questions. He's really that good.

As we spent a couple days together in his studio above his

garage, he walked me through the process of clarifying my own calling. One of the most profound insights I gained came when Pete said, *"Where your talents and your heart come together, this is where God has called you to be."* It's simple, but most of us miss it. God's gifts point to God's purposes. And when we allow those talents to intersect with the burdens God has placed on our hearts, therein lies our calling. Where your gifts and natural skills collide with your deepest burdens—you have *calling*.

As we sat together to reflect on my conclusions, we charted out the discoveries about my life on large sheets of paper suspended on his left-hand wall. Just below it, on Pete's cue, I took notice of at least thirty other rolled-up, rubber-banded pieces of paper collecting dust. "You see these rolls of paper?" Pete asked. "Every one of them represents a person who sat on this same couch. And when we really got down to it, most of these people were not ready to 'surrender' to what God had for them."

He went on to explain that the story line for many of the people he engages in this process ends early. They really think they want to know their gifts, talents, and calling, but when they arrive at some of the bold and challenging conclusions, they freeze. Their fear of failure, concerns for how they'll make money, and consideration of what others might think of them keep them from going all the way.

The next Christians are desperately searching for their calling. It serves *well* not only them but also those whom God wants to reach and serve through them. And this doesn't mean that their calling will always be a full-time job, as nice as that would be. For some, being a stay-at-home mother is the place where their talents and heart converge, and for others, their calling is found in service to their neighbors or local community or public school in a volunteer capacity.

* * *

WHEN SCOTT HARRISON returned to New York from his vacation in Mexico, he decided to become more exposed to the needs of the world. He followed his heart, not knowing where it would lead. For two years, he spent time on Mercy Ships in West Africa serving as a photojournalist, documenting monstrous tumors, cleft lips, and some of the most extreme physical needs that could be found in the world. He was utterly changed. His calling was being birthed.

Scott combined his *heart* for the poor in developing countries with his *talent* as a photographer, event planner, and entrepreneurial leader to launch a nonprofit organization. His vision was to create a charity organization that gave away 100 percent of its money and then used technology to demonstrate where it went. He simply called it "charity: water." His primary objective was to provide clean water for the poor. More than a billion people on earth have no access to clean water. Simply by focusing on providing clean water to poor, underserved communities, Scott's organization could positively affect everything, from education and economics to health and fighting disease.[10]

Scott was provoked by a problem, and he created a cultural good to solve it. He designed water bottles that sold for $20 each in department stores to fund clean-water projects around the world. And in less than three years, charity: water has raised more than $19.5 million and provided clean-water access for over 750,000 people in villages throughout Africa, India, and Central America.

As for Scott, he feels fully alive in this calling. He uses the talents and heart God has given him, and even the contacts and experiences from his past days of nightclub promotion. His new career doesn't even feel like a job, and he's never felt closer to Jesus.

This doesn't mean that you will love every detail of your vocation. Nor does it mean that pursuing your calling comes without sacrifice, times of weakness, and even failures along the way. I'm also not suggesting that every person's calling is to start a nonprofit organization to address a huge global problem. For you, it probably doesn't mean leaving your job or career at all. It simply means restoring right where you are.

The German philosopher Goethe offers these stirring words:

> Until one is committed there is hesitancy, the chance to draw back, always ineffectiveness. Concerning all acts of initiative and creation there is one elementary truth, the ignorance of which kills countless ideas and splendid plans: that the moment one definitely commits oneself, then Providence moves too. All sorts of things occur to help one that would never otherwise have occurred. A whole stream of events issues from the decision, raising in one's favor all manner of unseen incidents, meetings, and material assistance which no man could have dreamed would have come his way. Whatever you can do or dream you can—begin it. Boldness has genius, power, and magic in it. Begin it now.[11]

Perhaps you already know what God is calling you to do. You've envisioned how you can partner with God to be a restoration agent right where he's positioned you. If so, what's keeping you from going for it? Get up, get going, and begin now.

EIGHT

Grounded, *Not Distracted*

JASON EPITOMIZED A CULTURE-ENGAGING CHRISTIAN. LIKE A poster child for the forward-thinking believer we've been discussing, he dreamed of taking the Gospel inside the Hollywood film industry. Rather than wear the title of minister or evangelist, he planned to become an influential filmmaker. He even raised money, like a missionary, from friends and his local church to support his journey through film school—not just any film school, but the one at the University of Southern California, well known for its reputation of placing graduates at the highest levels in the entertainment industry. Jason knew God wanted him there, so he and his family waved good-bye to Fayetteville, Arkansas, and headed west.

Jason quickly garnered success at USC and he made incredible connections in the film industry while there. After two years of education, and a healthy dose of exposure to what was possible in the industry, Jason began to feel confident about his future.

As part of his strategy, Jason immersed himself in the Hollywood lifestyle, learning from directors, producers, and actors throughout the exclusive Beverly Hills community. His insider status gained him unhampered access to major social events in the City of Angels, where he rubbed elbows with the industry's movers and shakers. Needless to say, this type of "ministry" didn't seem to bother Jason much. The historic mansions, manicured lawns, boutique swimming pools, and personal drivers were a far cry from the environment of the typical frontline mission field.

All of this would have been just fine, except for one sneaky little omission from Jason's master plan: Christian discipline. I'm not talking about an inner moral will, or a code of religious propriety. I'm referring to the *practices* or *disciplines* that enhance and protect one's growing, authentic relationship with Christ.

On each rung of the Hollywood ladder, Jason had made small spiritual compromises: no consistent time listening and talking to God; no connection to the community of faith; no time searching the Scripture for God's wisdom; and no priority to protect his family. His heart and his passions were intact. But his plan lacked the structure that would have kept everything functioning. Jason was sort of like a house with no framing. And with less and less to hold up the Sheetrock and paint, Jason began to crumble.

Meanwhile, his wife, Cynthia, was trying to hold it all together. She had faithfully followed Jason's visions to become a leader in the film industry, but it wasn't without consequence. They had no extended family close by and very few Christian friends to offer support. And she could sense that Jason was beginning to drift. She would see it in his eyes and in the tiny indulgences that used to be off-limits. He began to nudge discernment aside to accommodate new friendships, and late nights became a venue for his changing cultural tastes. Jason began to justify any freedom he wanted in the name of full cultural exposure.

The idea of being a cultural missionary had paid his way through school, but now he was drifting in a different direction.

About that time, Jason got an enticing offer from a leading global advertising firm: They were tapping him to help launch a new division. He jumped at the chance. It was everything he had wanted, just wrapped in a different package. Sure, it wasn't the vision he originally had for making movies, but the job came with the income, platform, and niceties he had primed himself for. Jason accepted the offer and quickly succeeded. So much so that one of the world's largest retailers soon recruited him away to join their marketing department. They would be revamping their global brand and Jason would play a major role. He was a long way from the film industry now, but "success" was calling.

During his three-year journey back to Arkansas, first with the advertising firm, then with the mass retailer, Jason had decided to forgo everything to prioritize his career. Church was a relic and family dinners became a memory. Saturday mornings with the family was replaced with mandatory 7:00 a.m. company-wide meetings.

He soon grew close to his young, attractive boss, Shea. She understood his world better than most, empathizing with the demands that were placed on both of them. Office chatter became intense conversations, and before long, he was embroiled in an inappropriate relationship.

When their superiors caught wind of their affair, both were instantly fired, according to strict company policy. In a humiliating turn of events, Jason found his name plastered across the front page of the *New York Times* and *Wall Street Journal*. Within days, he had gone from being at the top of his game to becoming the scum of corporate America.

Jason ran. He left his family and fled his responsibilities. Cynthia and the children had followed Jason anywhere he wanted to go, but now he'd abandoned them. The seemingly harmless choices he had been making for years had now led to disaster.

*   *   *

JASON LIVED LIKE many talented Christians I've seen. Assuming they have the maturity to handle anything the world throws at them, they participate indiscriminately in every opportunity presented to them. But the consequences are often disastrous.

The next Christians must beware that operating in the center of the world requires a deep anchoring in Christ, a grounding that's achieved only through means unbecoming to most. Otherwise, it hardly ever works.

Stories of moral failure like Jason's are almost cliché. Together, they present another sad report on the state of Christianity and remind us that no matter how progressive our approach is to our faith, we're susceptible to stumbling.

Christians like Jason remind me of the biblical story of Daniel. Daniel was a person who pursued a disciplined life of cultural engagement but avoided being distracted by the very world he'd been called to restore. A young adult himself, Daniel lived some three thousand years ago when he engaged the godless and corrupt city of Babylon in the seventh century B.C. Let me give you some background and then explain.

Even as a youngster, Daniel was a pretty rare guy—known throughout the land for his intelligence and leadership ability. The Babylonians violently conquered the Hebrew people when Daniel was just a youth. After he was captured, specific orders were given for his immediate deportation eight hundred miles away to Babylon to be placed in service to the Babylonian king. Once there, he was enrolled in an intensive three-year retraining program designed to transform him into a loyal subject who would work personally for King Nebuchadnezzar (Dn 1). Daniel's special job placement came with some perks—the privilege of eating the king's meat and drinking his wine, an opportunity most people, especially a downtrodden captive, would jump at. It's not hard to imagine how he could have viewed this development as God's reward for enduring such a tough journey.

But because he was a Jew, this scenario presented quite a predicament.

According to Hebrew tradition, Daniel was forbidden to eat the king's meat, which had been offered to idols. Eating the meat was tantamount to validating the Babylonian gods, something Daniel knew deep down he couldn't do. If he relented on this one thing, it would represent succumbing to the world's ways. If he yielded, the pressure of his new context would have succeeded at breaking him down and superseded his original calling.

Daniel, being a clever leader, came up with a pretty risky, yet creative, solution. He persuaded his attendant to remove the meat and wine from his menu and to feed him and his Jewish friends water and vegetables for ten straight days. After ten days, if they showed physical signs of unhealthiness, they would subject themselves to the king's menu and risk death for rebelling by not eating the meat. But, if their disciplined practice—or, as it's become popularly known today, a "Daniel fast"—worked, they'd be in position to show a better way.

The lesson is critical. Daniel and his friends did something counterintuitive. They trusted that their faith would intersect with God's faithfulness.[1] They believed that following God's laws—remaining disciplined no matter the consequence—was important for them. They trusted that living God's way was better than the alternative. And they were right.

At the conclusion of the ten-day experiment, Daniel and his Jewish friends looked healthier than all the king's men. His attendant took notice. And their countercultural display changed the tune of King Nebuchadnezzar's mess hall. From then on, everyone in the king's service consumed water and vegetables.

Being grounded, not distracted, had paid off.

Success on the new Christian frontier looks a lot like Daniel's. By observing a few crucial practices, the next Christians are restoring brokenness without disconnecting from the Restorer himself.

PRACTICES THAT DISCIPLINE

Everyone is susceptible to the temptations and appealing nature of what the world has to offer. But the next Christians know that if they aren't disciplined, they risk sacrificing the greater work God may want to accomplish through them.

Jason's story may be an extreme one, but it broadly represents the many temptations the next Christians face as they try to live out their faith in a culture bent on success and achievement. In order to be restorers, they can't separate themselves from the world; they have to engage it and learn to live wisely as peers among their colleagues and neighbors.

From what I've observed, the next Christians invoke more than just wishful thinking when it comes to grounded engagement. They've learned that staying focused requires more than determination. Even a cursory reading of Jason's story offers solemn caution that *willpower* alone isn't enough to avoid the distractions.

So how do they do it? How do these Christians engage without falling prey to the temptations of the world? How do they show up in the grittiest of places without being offended or affected in a negative way? The answers are as old as the questions themselves.

Throughout the centuries, Christians have taken part in spiritual disciplines. A practice or discipline (I'll use the words interchangeably) in the Christian sense is something one does to become more like Christ, more of the person he made each of us to be. Historically, disciplines included things like fasting, prayer, Scripture reading, silence, and solitude.

Practices help Christ followers put more "self" aside, allowing Christ to live in them and through them, for the good of their own souls and for the benefit of God's redemptive and restorative purposes in the world. But it's not always easy. As Andy Crouch notes, a practice "starts out difficult, even positively painful, but over time becomes rewarding."[2]

Practices give Christians a way to hold strong to their convictions. In fact, practices are born out of conviction. But when our convictions wane, healthy practices keep Christians going. They restore us from our own wayward tendencies.

Of course, there are many general practices that people of faith have participated in for thousands of years—all are helpful for serious Christians to incorporate into their lives. People like Henri Nouwen, Richard Foster, Phyllis Tickle, Dallas Willard, and John Ortberg have written extensively and wonderfully on this topic, and I commend their work.

Nevertheless, the next Christians share at least five critical disciplines that stand out in our moment. They aren't necessarily more important than the others, but they carry more countercultural weight in our busy, distracted, disconnected, performance-driven culture. Because of that, these practices comprise, perhaps more than anything else we can do, how to be restorers in a culture that needs restoring. They seem to be oddities for the typical twenty-first-century American Christian. But these restorers have found them to be the grounding factor that allows them to remain pure, yet proximate to our changing world.

Let's look, first, at what for many Christians is the hardest of all.

Immersed in Scripture (Instead of Entertainment)

The average American spends almost three hours a day watching television.[3] That's almost an entire day, every single week, in front of the tube. Play that out over a life span, and it accumulates to almost *ten years.* Our culture is inundated with entertainment: television, video games, music, film, talk radio—most people spend more time on these forms of entertainment than on anything else except sleep and work. None of them are inherently evil, but the collective impact of their overwhelming presence in our lives has the ability to reshape our thinking and skew our perspective. Entertainment easily distracts us from our brokenness, diverting us from the deeper meaning of life by placating our senses as our lives slowly slip away.[4]

The next Christians' answer to this dilemma isn't simply to turn off the TV (though it's a good start). Rather, they've adopted a practice that counters the escape and buries them deep in real meaning, truth, and purpose. They have rediscovered Scripture and immerse themselves in it in a way that differs from the practice of recent generations.

To restorer-minded Christians, Scripture wasn't meant to be a science book, history text, or ethics manual, although they acknowledge it provides great insight into each of those subjects. They aren't determined to find verses to support their opinions or point of view. Instead, they enjoy Scripture as they believe it was meant to be: a grand narrative that tells a story of a God who loves and pursues, rescues, gives grace, and goes to any length to restore relationships with his most prized creations. Without robbing the Scriptures of their timeless, propositional truths, the next Christians are also rediscovering the thematic Hebrew stories of exodus and liberation, exile and return.

The next Christians are revisiting the jarring messages of Old Testament prophets who imagined a new world under God's reign. They are reengaging the narratives of Jesus's life and the early church as these Scriptures provide the foundational framework for God's plan of restoration for our world. Yes, along the way these Christians are made aware of their depraved condition and need for salvation, but they are also exposed to God's goodness inside them.

Many Christians may see this practice as an odd way to engage Scripture—and this bemusement only makes sense. For millennia, Roman Catholic Christians were not encouraged to read Scripture; the practice was looked upon with disdain (that's what the priest was for). It was just the opposite for many Protestants: Bible reading was seen as a daily duty, a task to be checked off before heading off to work or play. Once the

Scripture was available to laity, reading the Bible became an honor and pleasure. Similarly, the next Christians enjoy reading the Bible as much as curling up with a great novel. It invokes their imagination and instills confidence in a God who isn't just part of history but is showing up through them in their world today.

It gives them focus, but with a much bigger picture in mind. They don't encumber themselves with specific, and often legalistic, dos and don'ts (although these principles can be helpful); instead, they open themselves to learning and communing with the Creator.

A few new versions of the Bible seem to be popular with this group. Eugene Peterson's *The Message* is one of them. He wrote it as a paraphrase in modern-day language and, as such, removed the verse numbers and old English language that had made it unapproachable for many. Or consider how Chris Seay's *The Voice* project is recasting Scripture in terms of an interactive screenplay. All the while, institutions like Biblica have focused on reorienting readers to the literature styles and timelines within which Scripture was written. Their *Books of the Bible* version places each book of the Bible within its genre collection and then is ordered chronologically. And by removing chapter and verse it encourages smooth, uninterrupted reading of God's Word,[5] the way it was for centuries, before King James came along and made it a perceived requirement. These little (or major to some) tweaks are making Scripture come alive for a new generation of Christians.

Understanding Scripture is difficult. Passively watching television or quickly clicking through Internet links and Facebook updates is much easier. Engaging with our sacred texts takes time. And these Christians are making the time for it.

Observing the Sabbath (Instead of Being Productive)

Society today (at least in the West) rewards productivity and efficiency. We tend to spend most of our energy regretting what we haven't completed and being preoccupied by what we need to accomplish. In direct contrast, the discipline of practicing the Sabbath is all about ignoring yesterday *and* tomorrow—and being present in the moment.[6]

The term comes from the Hebrew[7] word *shabbāth*, meaning to cease, stop, or rest.[8] This ancient idea is rooted in Jewish and Christian tradition taken straight from God himself, who rested on the seventh day of creation.

But the Sabbath is bigger than just a way for *people* to be replenished and restored; it's meaningful for the creation itself. Even the experienced farmer practices this in how he rotates his crops. By God's design, fields need periodic time off from planting and harvest in order to replenish the nutrients that make them productive in future years.[9] The Sabbath "gives the world the energy it needs to live for another six days."[10] It is all part of God's original design for a good creation.

Recently, I decided to try practicing Sabbath. I'll admit it was difficult to embrace at first. Having three young children, a growing organization, and opportunities grabbing at me from all directions, practicing the Sabbath opposed my survival mind-set. I had "eaten the food" and unknowingly adopted the world's mentality that I was justified in stealing every waking moment to accomplish tasks, be productive, and get things done. Never mind what it was doing to my soul or those I loved most.

As I have begun to break away, my soul has been enriched. One day a week, I close my laptop, put the phone away, and play on the trampoline with my children. We blow bubbles, paint, make movies, draw Buzz Lightyear, play basketball, and have dance parties that would scare any onlooker. Rebekah ignores her to-do list. We read, laugh, and snuggle with the kids, taking in the simple pleasures that unbroken time allows. Sometimes that means a visit to the botanical gardens, a picnic by the lake, or enjoying the local art museum. Sabbath has become an intentional pause in our week to refocus and reclaim what matters most. And it reminds us that we are loved for who we are, not for what we can produce.[11]

Restorers understand how important and vital it is to take a break. This may seem like an archaic concept to many, but it's timely. It gives the next Christians a healthy way to disengage from a hyperproductive culture of efficiency so God can restore them.[12]

Fasting for Simplicity (Instead of Consuming)

The *idea* of self-denial is popular, but actually *practicing* it is altogether different. Historically, fasting meant to go without food for a period of time; but today, the next Christians apply this concept in almost every area of their lives where consumption can become an idol or a distraction. Fasting—whether not eating certain foods, not watching TV, buying less stuff, or intentionally escaping the magnetic force of online social networking—is providing a way for them to break free of earthly encumbrances. They are living more simplistic lives and it sets them apart from most of their peers.

Take, for instance, my friend Jeremy. He is a thirty-something single, creative professional, who recently gave up his virtual life during Lent, a forty-day Christian fast.[13] During that period, he didn't tweet or obsess about what new Facebook friends he could add to his online community. He disconnected and unplugged, and subsequently became aware of a few unhealthy habits in his life. First, he began to uncover how narcissistic he had become. The artificial value he was receiving from a booming online community of "friends" had all but replaced his deepest relational needs. Second, he discovered that his appetite for the Internet had driven him to waste precious hours of time every day. His fast helped him zero in on the much harder reality of being present with those around him.

Historically, fasting from physical needs "confirmed the Christian's utter dependence upon God, finding him as the true source of sustenance beyond food."[14] Fasting squelches the distractions, or as one friend puts it, "removes the veil" between the physical and spiritual worlds within which we exist.

The next Christians are finding that this practice leads them to much simpler lives. Our world finds comfort in *stuff*. We think we need newer clothes, bigger houses, and cutting-edge technology.[15] Fasting for intentional simplicity is a practice in breaking away. These Christians put themselves in the position of planned discomfort to deliberately experience simplicity in the most basic of ways.

Consider Chris and Phileena Heuertz. They have devoted their lives to serving the poor. They have sacrificed having a family and working in the comfortable atmosphere of being tenured college professors on a nice campus to place themselves in the world's poorest communities around the world. Their organization, Word Made Flesh (WMF), exemplifies how restorers are intentionally fasting from the comforts of this world to produce simpler, more grounded lives. WMF's tagline says it all: Serving Jesus among the poorest of the poor.

Practicing this discipline doesn't always mean selling everything and living among the poor, but it usually requires deliberate choices that don't always make sense to the average person. For suburban parents, it may mean committing to commute less than five miles from home for everything they need: groceries, the gym, school for the children. For others, it could mean cleaning out the clutter, buying only the necessities, giving stuff away, or downsizing their home.

Enjoying simplicity is counter to the message our consumer culture is barking from all angles. Society constantly tries to manipulate us into buying and consuming more than we need. Giles Slade, author of *Made to Break*, points out that this pressure isn't unintentional. In his book, he illustrates how entire markets have been built off of creating dissatisfaction with the old. Be it disposable diapers, razors, contact lenses, cell phones, houses, or televisions—our new landscape of consumption is based largely on buying products that quickly become obsolete.[16]

I see restoration-minded Christians bucking the trend. Instead of buying things they don't really need, they fast periodically from those habits that suck them in to this alternate reality. Certainly, this way of life often takes more effort and creativity on the front end, requiring their full imagination and a willingness to part with unnecessary comforts. But in the long run, they seem to be creating a more sustainable and less contrived existence.

However you apply the practice of fasting for simplicity in your life, you will likely contribute to a more thoughtful way of living that gives people a glimpse into what restoration is all about. By rejecting the status quo and fighting the manipulation to be like everyone else, you will demonstrate a better and more humane way to live.

Choosing Embodiment (Instead of Being Divided)

Over 20 million Facebook users update their status at least once each day, answering questions about what they are doing or what's on their mind.[17] The rest of us seem tethered to our cell phones, constant companions wherever we go. How many car accidents have you almost caused, only to look up and see the other party equally oblivious, phone stuck to his or her ear, locked in a conversation? Combine this with the latent pressure to respond quickly to e-mail, texts, and friend requests, or to update photos and online profiles while reading the rush of tweets and RSS feeds spilling into your in-box. We obviously live in a society full of divided people—or put another way, dis-embodied human beings. Our attention is distorted, our focus is skewed, and it seems to any casual observer that the days when a one-on-one conversation could be maintained (for more than five minutes) without one of these constant nags interrupting you are long gone.

Pastor Shane Hipps and a few other authors have uncovered the need for Christians to think seriously about how they manage technology, but imposing the discipline to do it is a whole different story. The next Christians have found a practice that is helping them to navigate this terrain. They are choosing to be embodied.

Visiting Kevin Kelly, a heralded futurist and senior writer for *Wired* magazine, at his home taught me a lot about embodiment. Kevin's work sits at the heart of technology innovation. If you didn't know him, you might assume he lives in a digital paradise—constantly online, voraciously keeping up with the latest new trends, a real mad scientist of sorts. But Kevin's life exhibits the complete opposite.

As we talked in his home office loft, the signs all around of his eccentricity and the nonconformist way he chooses to live refreshed me. He doesn't use a cell phone, has never twittered, rides his bike for transportation, and doesn't even own a laptop. Sure, he still has the attributes of a crazed inventor; we sat together underneath his hanging space models, alongside ant farms and amid mounds of clutter that evolves when an innovator does his best work. (Not to mention, I was greeted at his door by a ten-foot-tall Styrofoam robot, just as unusual as its inventor.[18]) But Kevin's simple life represents a complete anomaly; it's not how most of us would expect a futurist like him to live, and that's the point.

He represents a trait in the next Christians that stands out in our disconnected, technology-obsessed world. In what might be the most difficult arena to practice this discipline, he offers us a glimpse into how seriously these next Christians are committed to a restoration way of living. As Kevin explained in his own terms, this concept "comes from God's choosing to be embodied through Jesus, to enter into his own creation and relate to his 'creations' by being present with them. That's what I'm trying to mimic."

In a throwback to Daniel's famous fast, Christians like Kevin are finding that living an embodied life is giving them something more to contribute to the world than many other people have to offer. Eliminating meat is counterintuitive, but in reality less is actually more. This realization drives the restoration lifestyle of these Christians. They are living in the moment, practicing being fully present, always listening, always aware of the needs sitting right in front of them that go easily overlooked by others. They counter the numbness that overwhelms our society by being conscious of their surroundings and committed to solving problems that present themselves, often initiated simply by their showing up.

And while choosing embodiment may seem like one of the toughest disciplines to practice, Kevin has devised a few basic rules to help make it work. They seem to be useful for any Christian serious about this practice. He explains how he applies embodiment amid the onslaught of e-mail, phone calls, and demands of modern life:

> My first priority is face-to-face conversation. If I can be physically in front of someone, I give that person my full attention—ignoring competing distractions of phone calls or anything else that might hinder my focus. But if a face-to-face conversation is not possible, I defer to voice-to-voice—normally by way of the phone. But even with that, I have rules. When I'm having a phone conversation, I don't look at my computer screen or engage with anything in front of me, except the person I'm talking to at that very moment. I want to be fully present. But finally, if neither one of those options exist, my last resort is screen to screen. Using e-mail or sending a text is my last preference—but even then I keep it short and sweet but force myself to be fully present in the written communication I send.

As you can tell, Kevin is serious about setting priorities that help him be more embodied. He values true relationship and community. He's set his life up in such a way that he can fight the distractions and remain disciplined. His commitment demonstrates restoration in terms every Christian can learn from: by being fully present and disciplined enough to tune out the competing noise of society, Kevin can focus on others. And from multiple experiences with him, I can tell you he does it well.

Postured by Prayer (Instead of Power)

As culture drives the masses toward a me-centered existence, the practice of prayer is posturing the next Christians to remember who really sits at the center of their lives and faith. Prayer, by its very nature, settles the soul. In the most elementary descriptions of this practice, prayer is a way to bring our requests to God. But the deeper benefit is the way it changes the one doing the asking. Prayer humbles and postures the next Christians to recognize that they aren't in control or the primary ones responsible to "make it happen." It causes them to pause—just long enough—to recognize that their power comes from their connection with God and the working of his Spirit in their own lives.

This practice has always been a vital part of community life for Christians. A growing trend is the return to the millennia-old practice of fixed-hour prayer, an ancient ritual highlighted in the story of Daniel's faithfulness. Using the Book of Common Prayer, Phyliss Tickle's *Divine Hours* books, or applications now available on the iPhone, the next Christians are pausing at appointed times throughout every day to cease what they're doing and pray alongside believers around the world. It's a simple practice, but it requires intentionality and commitment.

No Christian believes prayer is unimportant. Unfortunately, our busy lives usually make prayer an afterthought—something we do quickly before a meal or resort to when we need God to intervene in a difficult trial. So how do we make it a priority? For me, community plays a huge role. I gather with a small group of guys every Thursday morning and we pray. We listen to one another's needs and hopes, then pray together and ask God to shape our response to our burdens and the brokenness of the world. It's a simple practice but creates in me a perspective that is necessary for God to work his will in and through me.

The consistent practice of these five disciplines goes a long way toward shaping the next Christians into the restorers God wants them to be. Most acknowledge that they don't always get it perfect, but they have been willing to reorder their lives to better posture themselves to participate in God's work in this world.

* * *

REMEMBER JASON AND Cynthia? Today they are back together.

The road has been long, hard, and painful, but after months of running, Jason came home. Cynthia stayed strong (and grounded). She prayed, sought God's wisdom, and relied on him to comfort her during this epic battle for Jason's heart.

Instead of abandoning Jason, his Christian friends embraced him. When he was ready to talk, they welcomed him in with open arms. These were his friends, the restorers that Jason and I have come to know. He'd hung them out to dry—used them for anything he could get—and left lifelong friendships in the wake. Yet they remained committed to him.

In the process, Jason admitted his wrongdoing and sought forgiveness from those he had hurt the most. As he began to get back on his feet, Jason reembraced many practices he had given up. He had learned his lesson in the hardest of ways and had the scars to prove it. He never wanted to go back to that horrific place and was determined to get back on track. He started being disciplined again, immersing himself in Scripture and prayer, and consistently fasting. His family began practicing the Sabbath and avoiding the distractions that had so easily confounded him.

His story about the perils of losing himself in the pursuit of the world is impacting others. Today, he shares authentically with cultural leaders all over the country, encouraging them with Daniel's lesson—don't eat the food, no matter what. He exhorts them to hold strong, stay grounded, and remain disciplined while they pursue their calling—or else.

Jason's life is the epitome of God's restoration project at work. The story doesn't end with Jason spending his next thirty years seeking approval and living a life of regret. He's been redeemed. His branding and marketing skills are being put to great use helping charitable organizations increase their impact. He's dedicated his life to serving others and giving a platform to their ideas through writing. He's abandoned his ambitious pursuit of success and put it all back in God's hands, knowing that God knows best how he wants to use Jason's life and story.

I recently invited Jason to join me at a U2 show in Atlanta. I had one more ticket in a friend's guest suite, and I knew how badly he had wanted to see their performance.

But to my surprise, he graciously declined. He told me how much he'd love to come, but he just couldn't do it without Cynthia. He had spent too many years enjoying rich experiences like this without his wife and he was determined never to do it again. We scrounged up one more ticket and they both came.

I can't imagine a better ending to Jason's story than seeing the two of them, arm in arm, soaking up U2's rendition of "Amazing Grace." They were two restored restorers. Grounded, in love, and on mission.

NINE

In Community, *Not Alone*

DAVID AND KATE AREN'T NATIVE TO THE WEST COAST. ORIG-
inally from a small town in the South, they moved to the Hollywood Hills after David began to pursue a serious songwriting
career. Today, he is a Grammy-winning musician, but when
they first settled in to show business, they were met with the
harsh realities of Southern California community—or the lack
thereof. After only a few months on the ground, they had
begun to experience the shallow isolation of a superficial city
where money talked and career-advancement meant everything. Los Angeles can become a harrowing city for outsiders.
If you can't afford the shopping, you're not a member of the
clubs, you're not pretty enough to get noticed, and you're no-
body's son, daughter, or close friend, then the only sure way to
fit in is to plunk down your $25 for a bus ticket on the stars'
home tour. This spread out, superficial, and sometimes just
plain unfriendly lifestyle isn't like the one they'd left behind.

Many in their situation would have accepted the culture for
what it was and leveraged it as a personal playground for their
success. But as restoration-minded Christians, David and Kate
felt acceptance wasn't an option. Rather than bemoaning the
dearth of friendships, they created a place where relationships

could be cultivated. They were provoked to counter the disconnected individualism by creating community.

Not long ago, I visited the Hollywood Hills to see how they were adjusting. After the suffocating drive from LAX, I knew I was nearing their home. As I headed up the steep drive known as Laurel Canyon, the road narrowed and the hairpin turns got tighter. On the left, two- and three-story homes were etched into the side of cliffs overlooking a picturesque scene of downtown Los Angeles. The homes were intentionally tucked away as if to shout "No trespassers" at anyone who might dare stop by unannounced.

When I arrived at David and Kate's home, however, the scene was different. Car after car lined the side of the mountain, jammed together in amateur-style parallel parking. It was typical of their Thursday-night scene.

When I walked into their home and dropped my bag at their door, my senses were overwhelmed. The smell of homemade lasagne filled my nostrils. A stranger welcomed me and offered me a cup of freshly made French-pressed coffee. The sound of friendly laughter overlaying Muse's latest album boomed from the iPod dock. People lounged comfortably on oversized chairs and couches, coffee in hand, engrossed in conversation about the profundity of life instead of the typical topics of fashion or gossip. The entire scene was a breath of fresh air. I knew I was in for a good night.

For David and Kate, creating community among their collective of friends is a nonnegotiable. They've learned that society's path tends to end in loneliness, emptiness, and, ultimately, disappointment. They'll do anything to fight that cultural tide—host the best parties, befriend new people, get involved in their local church, and find substantive friendships wherever they can. Without this community, they would be compromising the core of their faith. It's *that* foundational to how they live.

So most Thursday nights since they arrived in L.A., David and Kate have made it their habit to create an organic, communal oasis amid a sometimes unsympathetic city. No business cards are exchanged, name-droppers are ignored, and people come as they are—no pretense allowed. They informally refer to it as "family night."

They've broken through the ever-present facade of Hollywood, and made their house a haven of grace. Beyond this weekly get-together, they are constantly sharing their home with those passing through and giving of themselves to serve friends in need. They've created a community of friends that values doing life together, not alone. And it's been restorative in the purest sense.

* * *

ROBERT PUTNAM, SOCIAL scientist at Harvard University, comments that relationships have been moved to the back burner amid modern pressures. He says, "Neighborhood parties and get-togethers with friends, the unreflective kindness of strangers, the shared pursuit of the public good rather than a solitary quest for private goods" have strangely gone missing from American life.[1] Commuting, suburbanization, entertainment, financial pressure, time crunches, and an indifference toward civic responsibility in the next generation have created an isolated population.[2]

Experts describe the emerging societal environment as isolated "tribes of individuals."[3] Societal norms, such as encouraging people to prefer casual, uncommitted relationships to devoted ones, aren't helping. We seldom interfere in one another's lives; we don't have time, or maybe we just don't care enough. Instead, we hustle between work, friends, recreation, school, and church. We relocate frequently, and no longer have time to spend long evenings sharing stories with one another. Add to this our obsession with new technologies and the picture becomes clear: Most Americans subconsciously embrace cultural values that inadvertently destroy authentic community.

The social isolation and shallow personal connections may be easier to spot in bustling supercities like New York and Los Angeles, but many towns across America report the same symptoms. Under their polished surfaces, the drive for success and importance takes precedence over deep, committed friendships. People are left to fend for themselves in an ultimate game of "survival of the fittest" and often rugged individualism wins.

In stark contrast to today's social norms, the next Christians crave selfless, life-giving community. Like-minded individuals are assembling into affirming communities everywhere, and the next Christians are often at the helm. Intentional relationships define them. In essence, they are restoring community to its original place in culture.

These next Christians seem to recognize the irreplaceable role community plays in how we function as healthy citizens, and especially as Christians. As a result, they haven't bought the lie that individualism promises a better, more fulfilled life. They know that being grounded can't happen *without* a community of friends. They are a people committed to experiencing life together, not just by saying nice words but by engaging in the hard realities of loving, grieving, serving, and suffering with one another. They invite critique from friends and expose their true selves to others even at the risk of rejection.

*   *   *

As we've seen, being provoked to engage in a corrupted and broken world is a dangerous calling. The risks of such engagement can be tempered only by practicing disciplines that ground one in the way of Jesus. But it all falls short unless one is submerged in a vibrant community of faithful, loving, grace-filled believers. Community provides the critical support base the next Christians need to be on mission for God.

There's something special about communities that can soothe the brokenness in our personal lives. If you think about it, God could easily heal our ills and solve our problems. At the very least, he might eliminate them altogether from the lives of his most devout followers. But apparently, that's not his way. Instead, we need the support of others inside the context of a Christian community.

Interestingly, Scripture refers to this network of communities as the body of Jesus Christ.[4] In the physical absence of Christ, restoration continues through the work of the church— we are his hands and feet. And that paints a more beautiful portrait of his redeeming work than if God simply eradicated problems without our effort. It seems he would rather see us endure suffering *together* than see us thrive alone.

COMMUNITY RESTORES CHRISTIANS

The term "community" has a few different meanings. For now, I'll focus on one that's critical to how the next Christians support one another, and later I'll describe how this is affecting the way they are shaping the communities around them.

This first type of "community" may be defined as a group of friends united around a common goal. They are a group of committed people linked together by a purpose—like organizing a service project, fighting crime in a neighborhood, or learning about faith. The next Christians find this type of bond when they associate with other Christians pursuing the goal of faithfully following Christ. They've weighed the risks, counted the costs, and determined that without a committed community of like-minded friends, their hope to positively influence the world goes nowhere.

God himself validates this kind of community. As early as the creation of humanity, God saw that it was *not* good for a person to be alone. The creation story tells us that God created Eve to be Adam's companion, lover, coworker, and friend (Gn 2:18, 21–23). This wasn't a response to sin, but rather part of God's original design before sin entered the scene. God had "made humankind intrinsically suited for companionship and community."[5]

Jesus's ministry also demonstrates the importance of intentional community. He called disciples to follow him *together*—a group of people connected on a mission—and sometimes Jesus would even sneak away with just a few of his beloved friends like Peter, James, and John. Even though Jesus often retreated into the hills of Galilee for periods of solitude and prayer, he could usually be found sharing long meals with others or celebrating with family and friends.

But this type of community doesn't happen by accident. The next Christians are discovering a few ingredients that help them create this kind of kinship wherever they live. And in today's world, it's quite restorative.

Let's look at a few.

Relational Intimacy

Communities are built on trust and intimacy born out of deep connections. But relational intimacy often comes only after people show a willingness to be vulnerable about who they really are: their mistakes, bad habits, grandest dreams, and worst fears. I've found that intimacy flourishes when people are willing to "go there": when they are willing to share their wildest dreams and greatest hopes in the context of a group that genuinely listens and cares about what they have to say.

That doesn't mean the experience is always easy or feels good once they get the truth out. In community, their true friends call them out. By opening themselves up, they invite the healthy critique and accountability that help them become everything God intends—even if it hurts to hear. Having people who care about who they are and, most important, who they are becoming is a crucial component when pursuing God's purposes in their lives. Michael Metzger describes this dynamic as a "high intensity feedback loop,"[6] a place where people can bounce ideas, challenges, and dreams off a group of trusted friends who have their best interests in mind. In response, the community responds with honesty.

For David and Kate, hosting Thursday "family night" is only a small slice of their community. Most Sunday evenings they also congregate with a small group of believers with whom they share meals and explore matters of faith. Nothing is off the discussion table—philosophy, history, spirituality, loneliness, ambition, and temptations. Along the way, they've grown comfortable with exposing their true selves. When they screw up, they aren't handled with kid gloves; instead, their community challenges them to step it up and live better.

Emotions can be intense. Frustration, misunderstandings, and lack of discernment can quickly create awkward moments fast. But commitment to work it out is ever present in this kind of Christian community: they push through the pain when most people run, and enjoy what redeemed and restored relationships have to offer. Nothing like this kind of community exists anywhere else in the world, and it represents the best of what Christians can be.

Proximity and Permanence

One spring Saturday, I went with a group of friends to clean up Troy and Mazie Lynn's new backyard. They had just purchased an old rundown home with a severely overgrown lawn. In its current state, the house was uninhabitable. That was why we were there: to help make their home livable.

As we arrived and took in our surroundings, I was admittedly apprehensive. A crack house was visible nearby and sirens were blaring in the background. Neighbors peered from their own homes, suspicious at the new happenings at 147 Glendale Lane. Troy was using a chain saw to decapitate old wiry brush, and Mazie Lynn was carefully disposing of shards of glass and cigarette butts.

"Why would Troy and Mazie Lynn be moving here?" I cynically muttered.

The answer to my question became clear later that day. Bob Lupton, their mentor and soon-to-be neighbor, dropped by. We took an undeserved but well-accepted break. I sat down and rested on an overturned bucket, preparing myself to gain some perspective on all this.

Bob is an urban renewal legend. For thirty years he had

been recruiting families to live alongside him in East Atlanta, a forgotten part of town where few dared to live and others avoided at all costs. Troy and Mazie Lynn had given up the amenities of city life in a trendy, midtown location to take this on.

Troy and Mazie Lynn's choice to remain rooted is in stark contrast to the transient lives the rest of us lead. We change careers more often than ever before, and our jobs become an immediate reason to move. Even when they don't, we develop a "grass is greener" mentality that often prohibits deep community. Most people would never consider it part of being a good Christian to move to a city or neighborhood for an extended period of time—the concept seems too restrictive or committal.

Bob's strict belief in proximity and permanence drove them to make this decision. He believes that true restorative community, and ultimately positive change in the broader community, comes only when people intentionally choose to live alongside one another for the long haul.

But, living near one another in today's world can be hard, if not impossible. Richard Florida points out in his book *Who's Your City?* how little most Americans appreciate the monumental decision they make when they choose where they should live. In his opinion, the question of "Where will I live?" should be no less important than "Who will I marry?" or "What career will I pursue?" For Christians concerned about being *in community*, the decision of where to live isn't an afterthought or driven solely by the apartment or house they prefer. It's paramount to them being restorers.

Troy and Mazie Lynn weren't alone in their new venture. They were one of over thirty families who had decided to live in proximity to one another in this part of town. Committed to invest in one neighborhood and community for many years, they were part of an intentional effort to show the love of God to their community. They bore the mark of a textbook restorer.

COMMUNITY RESTORES THE WORLD

When community is working on all cylinders, the ripples of community touch *the world.*

As Americans, we are immersed in a society where independence reigns and individualism is our God. But it's galvanizing the opposite reaction. Instead of creating loners, the pendulum is swinging toward a deep craving for community.

Through just casual observation, you catch glimpses of this yearning all around. The "new urbanism" movement, for example, is growing in popularity. It boasts urban designs that feature wider sidewalks, expansive front porches, narrow roads, and green space for assembling and playing—at one time natural amenities for a community. New urbanists have even pinpointed the garage door as a "community killer."

Consider the popular advertising slogan used for planned communities: "Live. Work. Play." This language feeds an intrinsic desire to replace our commuter lifestyle with one that's less disruptive, a life where we more frequently encounter the people we live alongside. Our relationships need the oxygen of community to flourish. Think about your neighbor's enthusiastic participation in a homeowners' association, a book club, a tennis league, or the PTA—these are all great organizations to be involved in, but underneath the surface they each represent an attempt to quench the human thirst for deep and meaningful connections.

This brings us to the second type of community these Christians are encountering. In this sense, "Community" is the physical place where we all live—like a neighborhood, town, or city district—where multiple groups share the same public resources (schools, parks, city government, commerce, art, architecture, entertainment, and so on). For the remainder of this chapter, community (lowercase) is used for a group of people, and Community (capitalized) is used for a place.

* * *

THERE ARE FEW better examples of the principle of community restoring the world than the Clapham Circle first mentioned in chapter 6. Not only did they create the cameo that played a role in persuading public opinion to bring the British slave trade to its knees, but they were part of a community that encouraged and thrived on restoring the world around them.

Even among those familiar with William Wilberforce, few know about the way he remained connected to his community, the Clapham Circle. Wilberforce and his friends lived five miles outside of London in an area known as Clapham Commons for over forty years. Most of them were professed Christians, but the Clapham Circle community didn't just happen accidentally. It was due to an intentional choice they made to live in proximity to one another.

As the sociologist Clifford Hill points out, this "community did not come together at Clapham and subsequently begin to discover its identity. Members gravitated to Clapham in order to be near to those who were like-minded."[7] They chose to live together.

In Clapham, these friends regarded one another as family and "treated each other's homes as their own, taking with them as a matter of course their wives and children; they kept together for their holidays." They would meet in London for breakfast or dinner to discuss their shared concerns.[8] They didn't just socialize, but had a deep, kindred connection that was foundational for all that they would do together. This collective of friends made it possible for Wilberforce to spend forty years pursuing his two "Great Objects": abolishing slavery *and* reforming the manners (morality) of England. Today, over seventy reforms are credited to the Clapham Circle, from improving the living and working conditions of the poor to establishing the first animal humane society.

This kind of others-focused community, the kind the Clapham Circle demonstrates beautifully, is what the next Christians are creating for themselves. The manifestations of community vary among them, but a commitment to a service-oriented community that's grounded in mutuality is their common denominator.

Serving Others Together

The next Christians recognize that the most healthy community develops when they work together—usually in service to others.[9] When serving together—whether ministering to one another or those outside their community—they are forced to sacrifice, be inconvenienced, and demolish walls. They get to know one another in ways they wouldn't have to if they just sat around in a friendly circle talking. It is in the *doing* that they come alive, their gifts are exposed, and their hearts are opened to one another. Serving others together is the key ingredient in creating community.

Heather Locy does this well in the suburbs of Atlanta. Year

ᐧ

after year, she faithfully calls her community together to help meet the needs of the immigrant poor. Heather acts as an advocate for the immigrant population's underserved needs that often go unnoticed in the shadows of grander neighborhoods. Along with others in her church community, she has helped gather friends, coworkers, and neighbors to meet the needs of this unique populace. By organizing special events and recruiting people to volunteer, this faith community provides clothes, job opportunities, language education, transportation, and after-school tutoring for children in desperate need of support.

When communities serve together, they experience connection and purpose, and are reminded that this life is not about them. Serving is one of the clearest ways the concept of restoration begins to manifest itself in our world. Another is when these communities start participating in what's already going on in the broader culture.

Participation in the Wider World

One of the dangerous by-products of living in community can be separation. It's an unintended consequence of community. To counter this tendency, the next Christians intentionally overlap their lives and their service with the networks that already exist in the wider world around them. They are community leaders who bring their talents and skills to bear on any number of opportunities in the public square. As restoration-minded Christians, they plant themselves deep in their culture rather than parachute out of it (like Separatists sometimes do).

Rick McKinley models this concept well in the way he pastors Imago Dei church in Portland, Oregon. Instead of measuring its success based on Sunday-morning attendance, the church quantifies how many of its congregants are involved in restoring the city of Portland. He challenges his church community to put their gifts to use in service to their city. When newcomers attend Imago Dei on a Sunday, that isn't enough to be considered part of the church. They only gain that status when they've decided to apply their faith to a need within the Community.

Imago Dei church takes seriously the role of Christians to restore the world—from serving on the city council to volunteering in the public school or chairing the local arts festival. The church doesn't attempt to pull people out of their natural environment to serve the undeniable internal needs of a growing church organization. Instead, it empowers people to get involved locally by leading, serving, or creating—to bring the tangible love and goodness of God to their city in some way.

Many of the next Christians who are involved in more conventional churches are being forced to make a choice between the church or their Community. Some of Imago Dei's congregants spend less energy volunteering at their local church so that they have time to work serving the homeless in their community. Others choose to enroll their children in the local parks and recreation soccer league instead of a Christian league. Even the book you are reading represents this paradigm. I could have chosen to offer this project to a Christian Bookseller's Association publisher, but I decided to participate in the wider world by partnering with a respected New York publishing house. In some respects, a Christian publisher might have been easier to work with, but I wanted these ideas purveyed in the mainstream—not just among the Christian ghetto. The next Christians aren't content hanging out with their own. They are determined to participate in restoring the broader world.

It turns out that this isn't just good Christian practice; it's a historically proven way to advance their mission.

The historian and sociologist Rodney Stark observes that "social networks grow much faster when they spread through preexisting networks."[10] Citing the early church as a model, he notes that instead of creating their own institutions, Christians were known for joining and enriching existing ones. This made their faith less privatized and more engaging.[11] For centuries, Christians have been showing up in the middle of the world. Although recently, some have been sidetracked by a Separatist mentality, the next Christians are changing this by intentionally placing themselves in the middle of culture.

The Church as Community

So if these ingredients—intimacy, proximity, permanence, service, and participation in the wider world—are what really make up genuine community, where can people experience this today?

I've found it in restoration-minded local churches.

A healthy, functioning church can be one of the best places for this kind of community to be put on display. Despite what most people think, the "church" is more than just bricks and mortar. It's always been, and always will be, a fellowship of people that goes far beyond the walls of any building, denomination, or meeting space. It's a community of people who have found healthy patterns of human relating and new standards for how to treat one another, serve one another, and even forgive one another that run counter to the world.[12] These churches aren't always the most celebrated, and they come in all shapes and sizes. They meet in living rooms, coffee shops, art galleries, and typical church settings. But the bigger point is, the next Christians' churches see renewal and restoration as critical to their mission.

N. T. Wright describes a vibrant church community like this:

> It's a place of welcome and laughter, of healing and hope, of friends and family and justice and new life. It's where the homeless drop in for a bowl of soup and the elderly stop by for a chat. It's where one group is working to help drug addicts and another is campaigning for global justice. It's where you'll find people learning to pray, coming to faith, struggling with temptations, finding new purpose, and getting in touch with a new power to carry that purpose out. It's where people bring their own small faith and discover, in getting together with others to worship the one true God, that the whole becomes greater than the sum of its parts.[13]

This is how it was meant to be. God's strategy for the restoration of the world is carried out through this community called "the church."[14]

Regardless of whether your experience within one of these communities has been good or distasteful, it might be time to take a deeper look. The church, by design, is the place where support for restoration living should be felt most. And if you haven't found it yet, keep searching. Our team's work continues to reveal that this type of church represents the next major installation of the church in the West.

The church of tomorrow can't be identified by the architecture of their buildings or the styles of worship music they practice. Although many of them have a few similar qualities (like the ones described throughout this chapter), their most significant attribute can be found in the type of people they produce. You'll know it when you experience it. Full of grace and unconditional love for those unlike them, they don't obsess over recruiting people to be involved in their internal church programs. In fact, they probably don't have many programs because their lives are full with interactions throughout the community. They love Jesus and they show it through their genuine care for one another.[15] These small communities of faith, known as the church dispersed, are giving the world a comprehensive view of what it looks like for Jesus to show up in a *Community* today.

The next Christians get this. Having personally experienced the dangers of living life alone—from spending money they don't have to pursuing fleeting careers that distract them from who they were meant to be—they are committed to a better way. Instead of isolating themselves, they've plugged into the encouragement and accountability God intended. They decide to live in proximity to one another and often combine their resources to serve others. They have made the choice to be a part of a community that knows them, loves them, and wants the best for them. And in doing so, perhaps they stand a much better chance of staying aligned with God's intention for their lives.

Which might look different than anything you've ever imagined.

TEN

Countercultural, *Not "Relevant"*

CULTURES ARE LIKE CLOUDS. THEY MATERIALIZE AS BY-products of the prevailing conditions. They reveal the world's influential currents as they move across the landscape. And when you're inside them, it's hard to see what's really going on around you.

Even the most experienced cultural observers are struggling to forecast the future. Experts recognize that the changes are significant, but everything I've described so far is essentially a return to the roots of Christianity. What's so turbulent about that? Can something that sounds so elementary *really* be compared to monumental shifts like the Protestant Reformation or the Great Awakening? Is this really a pivotal moment for Christianity?

The reason I'm inclined to pound the drum so loudly is due to where we've been more than where we're going. The shift is important because it's such a dramatic reversal—a course correction—of where we've been headed until now. America was practically Christian just a handful of years ago, but in the past several decades, our country's predominant self-perceptions have been challenged and replaced. Moving at the speed of our ever-accelerating technology, society's ideals have evolved, removing its Christian underpinnings one by one. So although many of us still *feel* like we reside in Christian America, that reality is dead. Christianity once possessed an influential, "speaking for the masses" voice that tempered secular tendencies. Now that it's gone—as we reported in *UnChristian*—the reversed momentum is stronger than ever.

The next Christians refreshing personal "brand" doesn't merely fill a void of Christian inactivity, it replaces a negative brand that was somehow reflecting the opposite image of true Christianity.

Viewed from the perspective of the average person, this represents a radical reversal. It's like finding out that al Qaeda is really a relief organization with a few rogue leaders and a major PR problem. Or being told your whole life that raw pork can make you sick, only to learn that it's actually good for you—and can even cure cancer!

As we've seen so far, the next Christians are radically reshaping the Christian stereotype. Just to recap a few of the themes we've discovered along the way, these Christians are

> *provoked*, not offended,
> *creators*, not critics,
> *called*, not employed,
> *grounded*, not distracted,
> and live *in community*, rather than alone.

Taking a step back to consider how this plays in our current culture, it becomes clearer what is really going on within this new generation of Christians.

The next Christians are truly *countercultural*.

I know "counterculture" strikes you as odd, possibly conjuring up images of a muddy Woodstock, burning bras, gay rights activists, a lone figure on Tiananmen Square, anticapitalist anarchists, white-supremacist groups, or some other vision of an antimainstream movement. And that makes sense. Placing these Christians in that category wouldn't seem to fit—unless you really understand the kind of counterculture they represent.

But before we go there, let's debunk the myths that might prevent us from really seeing this for *what it is* and *what it's not*. Then we can explore the very specific way these Christians are being countercultural.

SEPARATIST COUNTERCULTURES

One trap Christians have fallen into historically in striving to be countercultural has been removing themselves entirely from culture. This is emblematic of the mantra of Separatist Christians—condemn and retreat. Removing themselves as far away from the corruption of culture is the name of their game.

The Amish are the most obvious. Although they are also a positive example of Christian faithfulness, they are an easy target for this label. For illustration's sake, let's consider how they have purposed to be a counterculture.

The Amish are confident in their beliefs about how the world should work and have created a lifestyle to facilitate it. They've separated from the world and could care less what anyone else thinks. Their deep belief in living within the rhythms of creation—from farming as their main trade to avoiding the use of electricity—guides many of their lifestyle choices.

They order their communities in such a way that they have no reliance on the outside world for anything. To them, letting the outside world into their community means danger. This was no more obvious than when someone from the outside world invaded an Amish community in Nickel Mines, Pennsylvania, in 2006 and horrifically murdered children in a small Amish school. It was the headline for days and for a brief moment the world was exposed to the way of life for these intriguing communities. To their credit, the Amish community met this single act of violence with an astonishing display of grace. Amazingly, the victims' families forgave the killer and even reached out to offer support to his family. Their reaction touched the hearts of millions of Americans. The irony, however, is that their display of true Christian virtue showed the great contribution the Amish counterculture could have in society if they just crossed paths with outsiders more frequently. They have much to offer our world, but few will ever be exposed to it because of their commitment to separate.

The lesson here is that Christians who remove themselves from the world in hopes of self-preservation miss out on carrying the love of God forward to those who might need it most. Separatism may indeed be called countercultural, but for the reasons mentioned, it's not the posture of the next Christians.

ANTAGONISTIC COUNTERCULTURES

I enjoy *Adbusters* magazine and read most issues cover to cover. I have always been intrigued by the way *Adbusters* uses its platform to prophetically call out rampant decadence, consumerism, and individualism. Granted, you might think some of the articles are over the top, and often they are. But they instruct us when we consider that they represent a very progressive counterculture today.

One of the founding publishers, Kalle Lasn, began this project in 1989 to fight what he describes as the pollution of the mental and physical environments in which we live. They have been phenomenal at recruiting what they call "culture jammers." These tens of thousands of supporters make their voices known in blogs, the walls of subways, shopping mall sidewalks, and wherever they can gain an eyeball to make the point.

The criticism to this kind of countercultural approach is that it is largely motivated by an anticultural attitude. Groups like Adbusters see little in current culture worth redeeming. They want to flip over the tables of society instead of negotiating the difficult terrain of working it out from within. By default, they are known for being great at pointing out the problems of society (albeit in sometimes offensive ways), but they rarely offer good or practical solutions and alternatives that promote a better way of life.

This condemning approach toward society represents a trap Christians often encounter as they seek to be countercultural. But it's a place these next Christians refuse to visit. In the days of Christian America, religious leaders were often better at cursing the darkness than lighting a candle. They became known for what they were *against* instead of suggesting alternatives that represent what they were *for*. (And I don't mean boycotting Disney and creating a Bible-themed amusement park to replace it.) This seems to be one of the most critical mistakes of engagement to date that Christians have made when attempting to be countercultural.

"RELEVANT" COUNTERCULTURES

In an effort to appeal to outsiders, some Christians copy culture. These Christians become a Xerox of what they perceive to be hip, thinking that others will perceive them as "cool." But trying to appeal to consumer wishes and pop culture habits is a recipe for disappointment for those trying to convey the Gospel of Jesus in society.

Consider the "Christian Music" section in your local bookstore. At surface level, it might appear countercultural. The lyrics are absent of obscene language and sexual innuendo. The artists unashamedly boast religious themes. But, of course, apart from worship music, the style largely mimics the same pop culture trends everyone else is following. It's not really a new genre; it's the same tired tunes with different words. Sure, they've achieved prominence by garnering their own section in the midst of "secular" stores. But that's not countercultural; it's just good brand strategy. It's a tribute to how well these Christians have separated themselves by copying the very thing they are trying to object to—the "consumer desires" of the wider world.

Taken a step further, an entire movement toward being "relevant" is running amok throughout American churches. Once a useful adjective, this word has become the idyllic Holy Grail for churches craving the cool factor. When they talk about being "relevant," they are describing their agility to adapt the message of Jesus *or* their ability to become like others in order to relate to them well.[1] The desire seems harmless, but relevance is the exact opposite of countercultural, and the unintended consequences are significant.

Just consider how this relevance mentality has swept up most Western evangelical churches over the last few decades. In the pursuit of relevance, many churches were deeply influenced by the business management theories of Peter Drucker, Zig Ziglar, John Maxwell, Jim Collins, and a multitude of others. Sure, principles of leadership transcend secular and sacred categories. But some pastors began to think *solely* of their churches as corporations and their jobs as CEOs. Their churches adopted the rules of commerce and subsequently became more driven by market and consumer principles than biblical ones. Numbers and pragmatics mattered more than anything else. This church-growth mentality has marginalized discipleship and true-life transformation for many who have encountered it. And ironically, those who have succumbed lost sight of Drucker's own admonition that "the purpose of management of the church is not to make it more businesslike, but to make it more churchlike."[2]

It didn't stop there. In recent times, the arts, entertainment, and media's overwhelming influence crept into the church: giant video screens, rock-and-roll worship music, and youth group rooms rife with video games. As the church began to mirror pop culture even more, the line between sacred and secular continued to fade.

Today, the latest influence on the pop culture–driven church is the push to be involved in social justice work. Many churches that have showed little interest in justice work before are now simply following the latest social fad. They need to draw in a younger crowd, so social ministry has become another way to appear relevant.

Taken to its logical conclusion, the pursuit of pop-culture relevance creates an endless cycle that removes the church

(Christians) from its historically prophetic position in society. But Christians who have grown frustrated with their loss of credibility in the public square see relevance as their method to bridge the gap. They think, "If we can make Christianity cool again, everyone will want in." Admittedly, every one of us wants to be liked, accepted, and respected by our peers—that's normal. But unfortunately, with this view, these Christians overlook the inherent problem in their attempt to relate to culture—trying to be relevant makes them cultural *followers,* not cultural *leaders.* It's a catch-up mentality. The pursuers end up in second, third, or fourth place, striving to be in the lead, but never quite getting there. It's proving to be a misguided premise.

Yes, of course, we must contextualize our message, and this book is partly an attempt to call Christians to recognize and respond appropriately and faithfully to the cultural changes that are taking place. But the church should be offering an alternative way of living and being that stands out in a confused and broken world, not simply copying what it sees.

Recently, I had an enlightening conversation with Kristi that sheds some light on what's at stake. At the age of seventeen, she had grown up in the typical church youth group. The relevance mind-set had influenced their church space, lined with televisions and video games, to look weirdly familiar to her friends' basement hangout. In the attempt to relate, the youth group had turned into an entertainment venue trying to attract and keep the attention of teenagers.

She was done with it.

After all these years, she was looking for something deeper. She craved truth, meaning, and purpose. No longer content with pizza parties and lock-ins, she longed for a faith with credibility that matched her real-world longings.

As fate would have it, she began dating a Mormon.

As Kristi got to know him, she was intrigued by his odd practice of spending early school mornings at his local church studying the Book of Mormon. Five thirty a.m. comes early. For her, it spoke to something deeper. She was drawn to his commitment and self-sacrifice. He was one of the brightest and most thoughtful peers she knew. His church community demanded much from him and he was responding.

This stood in stark contrast to anything she had experienced in her pursuit of the same. Kristi had hardly encountered this type of devotion among Christians she had known. As she put it to me rhetorically, "Would I rather go to a pizza party or study church history and pursue answers to my deepest spiritual questions?"

She was convinced. Relevance in terms of what pop culture deems cool meant nothing to her. So she began to pursue Mormonism.

In her case, and probably for many others, her church's pursuit of relevance created the unintended consequence of reducing the demands on the call to be Christian. The commercialization of the message has limited, covered up, or perhaps even thwarted the deep and penetrating impact the Gospel can have on people's lives.

Simply put, relating to the world by following the world can be a recipe for disappointment and disillusionment.

Countercultures that point out the problem but offer nothing as a solution ultimately fail in their mission. And pursuing relevance at all costs isn't countercultural at all.

The next Christians are living in the tension of being prophetic with their lives while serving others and inviting them to a better way.

A COUNTERCULTURE FOR
THE COMMON GOOD

Placing the label "countercultural" on the next Christians may seem counterintuitive at first. When I initially discovered this characteristic about the movement, it struck me as odd as well. But the longer I've studied this concept, the more it makes sense as a promising development for the future of Christian life in the West.

In contrast to countercultures that separate, antagonize, or copy culture, the next Christians are a *counterculture for the common good* that is centered and immoveable. They don't concern themselves with popularity, what they can achieve for themselves, or whether the masses are following. Instead, they boldly lead.

Preserving Agents in a Decaying World

Sin has corrupted every aspect of our world—from devastating hurricanes, earthquakes, and decaying trees to the depraved hearts and minds of humankind. Since sin entered the world, our relationship with God, with our own self-identity, with others, and even with creation at large is broken and corrupt. The apostle Paul even speaks about creation itself as being in "bondage to decay" (Rom 8:21).

Many Christians, however, are tempted to believe God is only concerned with saving individuals while our world spins out of control on its predestined path to destruction. In contrast, Jesus seemed to offer a more complete vision.

Christ said, "You are the salt of the earth. But if the salt loses its saltiness, how can it be made salty again? It is no longer good for anything, except to be thrown out and trampled underfoot" (Mt 5:13). For ages, salt has been understood as the key agent for preserving and protecting food from decay or spoilage. This was especially true in the ancient world where the modern technology of refrigeration didn't exist. Jesus likely used the idea of salt to define how his followers should interact in the world.

Salt is only useful when it's good, active, and engaged—doing what it's supposed to do where it's supposed to be. Salt doesn't preserve anything by itself; it must attach to something in order to provide its life-sustaining and preservative value. Left on its own, even in proximity to meat, salt will do nothing to keep the meat from going bad. And meat left alone, without salt, will rot and be rendered useless. But when the two intermingle—when the salt is rubbed deep into filet mignon—it not only preserves the steak but expresses its greatest attributes in taste, quality, and flavor.

The next Christians see themselves as salt—preserving agents actively restoring in the middle of a decaying culture. They attach themselves to people and structures that are in danger of rotting while availing themselves of Christ's redeeming power to do work through them. They understand that by being restorers they fight against the cultural tide. But they feel called to restore and renew everything they see falling apart. Although they know they may never see the full manifestation of their work, they honor God by living in this way. Their commitment to hold back evil, to repair systems and structures, and to heal people who are broken and suffering from the fall gives an alternative trajectory to the average life.[3] They bring peace to situations and are constantly about the work of putting things back together.

Rather than fighting off culture to protect an insular Christian community, they are fighting for the world to redeem it. This is the essence of being countercultural for the common good.

Pursuing an Inverted Lifestyle

Mother Teresa was one of the poorest saints in the world—but she was given the world's stage with moral authority very few possess to sound off against abortion. To this day, she is still referenced as one of the holiest people to live in the twentieth century. There was a time, however, when Mother Teresa was just a common nun. She was not always a religious icon, and her rise to prominence illustrates that everyone has the potential to recognize the way of Jesus. But it only starts when Christians recognize and embody what Jesus actually taught:

> *Blessed are the poor in spirit,*
> *for theirs is the kingdom of heaven.*
> *Blessed are those who mourn,*
> *for they will be comforted.*
> *Blessed are the meek,*
> *for they will inherit the earth.*
> *Blessed are those who hunger and thirst for righteousness,*
> *for they will be filled.*
> *Blessed are the merciful,*
> *for they will be shown mercy.*
> *Blessed are the pure in heart,*
> *for they will see God.*
> *Blessed are the peacemakers,*
> *for they will be called children of God.*

> *Blessed are those who are persecuted because of righteousness,*
> *for theirs is the kingdom of heaven.*

(MT 5:3–10)

This sums up well the essence of the Christian call to a countercultural life. A God-centered life is a counterintuitive existence that flips the values of the world upside down. It's an inverted way of living that reverses the importance of what the world tells us to value most. The Western inclination is to chase after wealth, comfort, power, happiness, success, and the ever-sought-after American dream. But Jesus is describing an alternative way of living and engaging that flies in the face of these values. And just to drive the point home, he instructs those who claim to follow him with the most extreme commandments:

> Love your enemies, do good to those who hate you, bless those who curse you, pray for those who mistreat you. If someone slaps you on one cheek, turn the other also. If someone takes your coat, do not withhold your shirt. Give to everyone who asks you, and if anyone takes what belongs to you, do not demand it back. Do to others as you would have them do to you.

(LK 6:27–31)

This is the inverted way God's economy works. It runs counter to what the world values in all of its selfish, humanistic ambitions. When someone betrays your trust or stabs you in the back, your natural inclination is to make him or her pay. When your character is impugned or someone attempts to ruin your reputation, you want to attack back and gain the upper hand. But Jesus challenges his followers to seek a different "upper hand," a "lower hand" if you will. We should be models of very countercultural values. As author Eugene Peterson points out, "we follow a very different leader, one who in virtually every detail guides us in a way of living that is counter to that of the world."[4]

The next Christians have rediscovered this ideal. They don't always get it right, but they are seeking to follow the way of Jesus wherever they show up. And as they try to faithfully live in this way, they paint a picture to a curious world of an alternative way of living. Their lives are pointing to a better way forward for those inquisitive enough to notice. And seeing this kind of commitment to the faith in action can be quite appealing for the average onlooker.

Making Sense of the World

When I lived in Atlanta, I would often fly to New York City for meetings—sometimes up and back in the same day. Anyone who travels there frequently knows to map out his transportation plan ahead of time: which airport to fly into, the time of day to avoid gridlock traffic, and which train line to take into Manhattan.

For me, this meant getting up early and catching Delta's first flight into La Guardia Airport. Once I deplaned, I'd get in the taxi line to wait my turn. If you've ever been to La Guardia, you can appreciate the scene. Out the doors and a glance to the right exposes you to a sea of yellow: hundreds of cabs lined up, drivers hanging out waiting for their turn to cash in on a $40 fare into the city. The line moves quickly as a constant flow of arrivals jump in cars, state their destination, and head to their first appointment.

Almost every time I'd leave the airport and take a cab toward the Triborough Bridge, I'd notice a strange experience happening on a slightly isolated corner of the sidewalk. Anywhere between five and ten faithful Muslims, turbans on, lay prostrate on their prayer mats facing east. Whether it's ninety-five degrees or sleeting ice, these men were committed to practicing their faith while on the job awaiting their next assignment.

What intrigues me, though, is how committed these men are to their way of life. For me, it piques a genuine curiosity. I want to know more, to understand what is motivating them to be so faithful to such a culturally odd practice in the public parking lot of an airport. Even though I don't fully get it, and even though I've never felt the need to pray like this in public, I respect their countercultural commitment. The *odd* and *curious* practice of seeing a grown man put his face on a rug in the middle of a parking lot makes a statement. It says, "I'm serious about my faith. I'm committed to expressing it and don't care what anyone else thinks. I've found a better way to live!"

And this is true of the next Christians. Although you likely won't find them on prayer mats in the middle of a parking lot, they believe just as passionately that they have discovered the best way to live. They're proud of it. And others seem genuinely curious about what it is that is motivating the change.

They certainly don't flaunt it in the faces of those who aren't as far along on the journey. They simply live it out and invite others to join in along the way. They live with gratefulness that they've providentially stumbled upon a better, truer, alternative way of life. Taking seriously their responsibility to embody the Gospel, they trust the Holy Spirit to work through them in his time to persuade others to join up. Occasionally, that leads to others' choosing to become Christian and pursue the journey alongside them. At other times, it sheds light on a new way of being Christian to which they'd never been exposed.

Maybe you've heard some of their stories throughout this book and created your own perception that these Christians, as countercultural as they are, still seem quite hip. It's a bit understandable, but don't be confused by the simple distinction. Labeling someone "relevant" is a subjective tag, usually just a matter of style; but it's the substance of these Christians' commitment to restore that's driving the curiosity of the world.

I can think of no better example of this than Shane Claiborne. As an activist-turned-author, Shane embodies this countercultural lifestyle. Living in a communal house on Potter Street in the Kensington neighborhood of urban Philadelphia, Shane chooses not to own a car. Not because he can't afford it, but because he believes it would place his level of material possession above that of his neighbor. And in his view that's not showing love at all.

He's a radical by most people's standards. He travels the world in John the Baptist–style hand-sewn clothes, doing anything he can to fight injustice, stand for peace, and genuinely love others. This has taken him everywhere from the streets of Baghdad during the initial Iraq War bombing campaign to planting a community garden in his neighborhood. Though some people disagree with Shane's theology, no one would question his commitment. Shane cares about people.

He lives out his first commitment of following what he understands to be the way of Jesus and restoring anything broken that presents itself along the way. And when he does, the world's curiosity is piqued.

Shane was featured in *Esquire* magazine as one of their "Best and Brightest."[5] It's not his long dreadlocks that are drawing the interest, but his oddness to believe that Jesus's way is a better way for the world. He's a Christian who has radically changed the order of his life to align with the ways of Jesus. People are curious to know what drives someone like Shane to live in such a countercultural way. They are responding to the substance and to a man whose life authentically models their greatest hopes. I think deep down most people long to have such a willingness and humility to submit to live in a better way—but it takes people like Shane to open their imagination that this kind of life is even possible.

Christians like Shane represent the type of people and lifestyles that fly in the face of the values of contemporary culture. You may not feel called to make your own clothes or protest war by placing yourself in harm's way, but as a Christian, when you restore where you are, people take notice. You become the model of a person who pursues deep relationships, lives with purpose and meaning, commits to the service of others, and reconciles injustices wherever they exist. If you strive to be faithful to Christ, your life will paint a picture of what every human soul is longing for. In turn, the world will take notice that this way of being Christian might just be a better way.

These countercultures are changing the face of Christianity in our world. No longer embarrassed by false representations of the Gospel, the next Christians are communicating something authentic and true through their lives that gives pause to those who encounter them. By being faithful to how Jesus calls them to live, they offer an attractive alternative for the spiritually hungry.

* * *

ONE RIVETING EXAMPLE can be found in Portland, Oregon—a proudly liberal place known as one of the most un-churched cities in North America. I've known that leaders in Portland have been praying and working together on various projects that affect their city for years, but now the tremors have reached the surface.

On behalf of several hundred churches, world evangelist Luis Palau and his son Kevin met with Portland's mayor to ask a simple question: "How can we serve for the good of the city—no strings attached?" Local pastors and Christian leaders were taking seriously Jeremiah's challenge to "Seek the peace and prosperity of the city to which I have carried you" (Jm 29:7). They had work to do to repair the church's storied relationship with this Northwest community and they were willing to go to any length.

They got specific and the answer was clear and concise. Five areas were identified for further exploration: homelessness, hunger/poverty, health/wellness, public schools, and the environment. The church responded.

Portland's small but committed Christian community caught a vision for their city and began to raise up volunteers. Season of Service was born. Within the first year, 450 congregations and 28,000 individuals were enlisted in the cause. They established a dozen free medical/dental clinics to serve the area's uninsured and launched Home Again Mentoring Plan, a program providing long-term mentor teams for homeless families. Portland was so impressed with the work being done, they even allowed churches to begin "adopting" public schools. In a city where the Christian community had little influence, churches are now seen as a powerful force for long-lasting change.

Portland's mayor Sam Adams—the first openly gay mayor of a major U.S. city—has publicly praised the initiative and offered his full support for three consecutive years. As he issued the official declaration for Season of Service '09 in front of five hundred pastors, he gratefully explained, "When we first heard the idea . . . we were skeptical, but our modest hopes were incredibly exceeded by what you and your churches accomplished."[6]

During that same meeting, leaders representing more than three hundred churches presented the mayor with a gift of $100,000 to help reduce the high school dropout rate and mentor those in homeless families. While some churches may have used that money to start a new program or launch a building campaign, these churches gave it away. They are praying that this is just the beginning.

The media has taken notice as well. An editorial in *USA Today* praised the "stereotype-busting sub-plots . . . the most intriguing of all being the way the Season of Service has thrust the area's Evangelicals into partnership with the city's most liberal leaders."[7] *Willamette Week*—Portland's alternative newspaper—surprisingly noted that the church community "has moved its unashamedly evangelical operations into the most secular of cities with nary a peep of protest."[8] Even *Reader's Digest* listed Season of Service in their Best of 2009 issue, naming it one of the nation's best community service initiatives.

The people of Portland are being refreshed by a new brand of Christianity. Rather than retreat into their churches and conduct business as usual, these restoration-minded Christians engaged their city as the countercultural hands and feet of Jesus Christ. Over time, the church has earned a seat at the table. They are included in serious discussions about the future of Portland and illustrate well the difference a countercultural community for the common good can make on the place they call home.

*   *   *

THE NEXT CHRISTIANS try to create the most good for all people, regardless of race, class, or religion. Christians shouldn't strive for what's best only in their own community of believers, though that's important. They should concentrate on the benefit of all people in God's creation whether or not they share our values, ethnicity, or religion. As Tim Keller reminds us, "Christianity will not be attractive enough to win influence except through sacrificial service to all people, regardless of their beliefs."[9] As Christians, we must work for the peace, security, justice, and prosperity of our neighbors.[10] We have a responsibility to be in service to the good of our cities while we remain grounded in Christ. For the next Christians, these two are inseparable.

The Christian approach, then, is one that should offer a better way forward, one that is more constructive and in line with how the Christian perceives God's original intent for his creation that values both human life and a flourishing creation. As the theologian Cornelius Plantinga points out, "central in the classic Christian understanding of the world is a concept of the way things are supposed to be. They ought to be as designed and intended by God, both in creation and in graceful restoration of creation. They are supposed to include peace that adorns and completes justice, mutual respect, and deliberate and widespread attention to the public good."[11] This is what it means to exist for the common good.

But that doesn't mean it will always be easy—or that the world will at first glance appreciate the countercultural nature of what's being proposed.

Going against the ebbs and flows of culture can create friction and sometimes provoke a hostile reaction to the good we are trying to create. Theologians Stanley Hauerwas and Will Willimon remind us that this should be expected, for "whenever a people are bound together in loyalty to a story that includes something as strange as the Sermon on the Mount, we are put at odds with the world."[12]

However, living in contrast to the world doesn't mean we have to lack credibility. As the apostle Peter says, "Live such good lives among the pagans that, though they accuse you of doing wrong, they may see your good deeds and glorify God on the day he visits us" (1 Pt 2:12). This is the epitome of being countercultural for the common good.

Nothing illustrates what's possible better than an anonymous letter written to Diognetus, a Roman scholar who lived between the second and third centuries (likely during the great persecutions of Christians). It shows the tension—and the potential—of how thinking and living with a restoration focus can impact the world.

> The Christians cannot be distinguished from the rest of the human race by country or language or customs. They do not live in cities of their own; they do not use a peculiar form of speech; they do not follow an eccentric manner of life. . . . Yet, although they live in Greek and barbarian cities alike . . . and follow the customs of the country in clothing and food and other matters of daily

living, at the same time they give proof of the remarkable and admittedly extraordinary constitution of their own commonwealth.

They live in their own countries, but only as aliens. They have a share in everything as citizens, and endure everything as foreigners. Every foreign land is their fatherland, and yet for them every fatherland is a foreign land. They marry, like every one else, and they beget children, but they do not cast out their offspring. They share their board with each other, but not their marriage bed.

They busy themselves on earth, but their citizenship is in heaven. They obey the established laws, but in their own lives they go far beyond what the laws require. They love all men, and by all men are persecuted. . . . They are poor, and yet they make many rich; they are completely destitute, and yet they enjoy complete abundance.

To put it simply: What the soul is in the body, that Christians are in the world.[13]

The next Christians might be countercultural, but could they possibly be the answer to restoring the soul of our world? We'll wait and see.

For now we know that the clear call of Jesus is for the Christian community to be salt and light. Not simply a bunch of small lights in all the dark corners of the world, but a communal light that provides a picture to the world of what a loving, sacrificial, countercultural community really is. It's a collective of people living by a different standard—raising the bar and inviting everyone who's interested to join in.

PART III
A NEW ERA

ELEVEN

The Next Big Shift

THE CHRISTIAN MOVEMENT IS ENTERING A TIME OF TRANSFOR-
mation on a par with the Protestant Reformation. In *The Great
Emergence,* Phyllis Tickle illustrates a pattern of historic changes
taking place among Christians every five hundred years. If this
pattern holds, our faith is on the cusp of a massive shift.

Tickle, author and founding religion editor for *Publishers
Weekly,* says the first shift began almost five hundred years after
Christ's death when the Roman empire fell and with it, Con-
stantinian Christianity. Five hundred years later, the Great
Schism of 1054 divided Roman Catholicism and the Orthodox
Church. Finally, in 1517 the Reformation gave rise to Protestant
Christianity.[1] With history catching its stride, the movement
seems primed for the next iteration of Christian practice.

The end of Christian America has pushed us into a new era
of faith, one marked by believers that possess the six characteristics I've described. Our current metamorphosis will doubtlessly
bring its own challenges and successes, much like the other great
shifts. Yet the faith will survive as it always has. The people of God
will continue forward as they've been doing for two millennia
so long as we keep the foundations of our faith grounded in the
Gospel of Jesus Christ. This is of first importance.

FIRST AND SECOND THINGS

Too often we confuse first and second things. If I want my children to have beautiful imaginations (a second thing), I must first turn off the television, read them descriptive, fantastical books, and give them experiences that let their minds wander and dream (a first thing). I can't tell them to practice "imagination." I have to create an environment that first encourages it. Consider bestselling books. Authors don't set out to create a bestseller (a second thing), and in most cases if they did, they'd never get the result. Instead, they set out to write an honest account of their view of the world (a first thing) in hopes that others will appreciate it and benefit from it. If the readers tell their friends and more people read it, the book could become a bestseller. But you hardly ever achieve the second things without first focusing on first things. As C. S. Lewis wrote in his brilliant essay "First and Second Things," "You can't get second things by putting them first; you can get second things only by putting first things first."[2]

* * *

AT JUST EIGHTEEN months, my daughter Kennedy Rose was successfully navigating the terrain of her older brothers and discovering profound life truths. Late on Christmas Day her elder of two years, Pierce, had staked claim to *her* favorite Christmas present—a red Little Tikes car (one big enough to sit in). Kennedy was not happy. After the enthusiasm of opening presents had worn off, she had fallen ill with post–Christmas morning funk. Generosity had subsided and selfishness reigned. Pierce had taken up residence in her new car, and she was having nothing to do with it. This was her car, she wanted it back, and that meant Pierce had to go.

With less than twenty words to her vocabulary, she modeled for me a lesson that's proven to be ostensibly true in every area of my life. In an attempt to persuade Pierce to get out of the car, she begged and pleaded with him. When she realized this wasn't working, she pulled at his shirt, which only made matters worse. Her growing aggravation was clear, but she wisely stepped away to ponder her options for a moment (as all good eighteen-month-old girls can do). If her objective was to get her car back, she'd have to change her approach.

In a moment of genius, she took off for the living room and returned proudly displaying Pierce's most prized present from that same Christmas morning: his Thomas the Tank Engine. She came close enough for him to see it and then proudly announced her intention: "I pway with twain."

Within two seconds, her problem had been solved. Pierce leaped out of the car to pull his train out of his sister's grasp. In a moment of perfect manipulation, Kennedy made a seamless exchange. She let go of the train and slipped into her car, harboring the most mischievous grin I'd ever seen on her face. Pierce glanced back, dumbfounded that he had given up his prized seat with no idea how it had happened.

Kennedy had learned one of the most important truths in life: Getting the result you want often happens only when you properly order first and second things. In her case, the first thing was persuading Pierce to play with his own toys (albeit not willingly). The second was getting to play with hers.

* * *

THE FIRST THING for the Christian is to *recover the Gospel*—to relearn and fall in love again with that historic, beautiful, redemptive, faithful, demanding, reconciling, all-powerful, restorative, atoning, grace-abounding, soul-quenching, spiritually fulfilling good news of God's love. As described throughout the earlier chapters of this book, it is critical that this come first.

Following Jesus in the twenty-first century demands that his disciples relearn the full meaning of the Gospel story, recovering the culminating theme of restoration that runs throughout the whole of Scripture. This begins by seeing the Gospel as the central resolution to humanity's age-old questions and self-conflict. But this story isn't static; it dynamically continues to unfold today, displaying God's original goodness and ultimate intention for all his creation. The good news for humankind is that we are all made in God's image, given a path through Jesus to be reconciled from our sin, and purposed to partner with him to renew and restore the creation to its fullest potential.

Christians can easily get sidetracked with distractions. And most of the time, those diversions really amount to second things in the form of debates, programs, and methodologies that can cloud what matters most and are easily worked out when first things are put first. Outreach methods, good deeds, social justice, cultural engagement theory, church models, environmental stewardship, career paths, even the negative perceptions of Christianity are some of the most current and popular distractions. But these represent second things for the church. They seek to distract, compete for the center, and manipulate us into believing they're really the main thing. But they're not. The restorative work of Jesus as displayed through the Gospel *is* the main thing—indeed, the one and only and true first thing.

This truth of the Gospel should illuminate Christian focus in the coming century. Unconcerned with outcomes, Christ's followers must get back to the heart of their faith—recovering, relearning, and rebuilding from the core first, and then out. I realize this may sound too simple for some. But it's likely that the greatest results will come from returning to the tried, true, and foundational truths of the faith. As I see it, and have tried to illustrate throughout this book, a new movement within the Body of Christ is underfoot. But the biggest challenge that lies ahead will be Christians' ability to hold tightly to their first thing and let everything else take care of itself.

*   *   *

AT FIRST GLANCE, the mind-set of restoration we've been discussing may appear to contrast with the conventional Christian outlook that emphasizes personal salvation and discipleship. But the opposite is true. In addition to serving the physical needs of the world, the next Christians are also seeing their friends, neighbors, and colleagues come into relationship with Christ. I'm talking about authentic salvation and discipleship experiences. The radical nature of restorative living incites others to ask questions.

The fact is, where Christians restore, people get saved. And the perception these new converts have of what it means to be Christian is pure and unmistakable. When someone's introduction to Christ comes through an encounter with real grace, love, and an invitation to a better way, it's likely to reproduce in them the same result. The Holy Spirit works in the hearts of

men and women when they encounter the Gospel lived out in
real ways. This isn't some new strategy—it's the way Christianity
has flourished ever since it began.

Christianity grew by some 40 percent in each decade during the first three centuries after Christ. As described in the
letter to Diognetus, these Christians were involved in the fabric
of society, constantly restoring and demonstrating a better way
to live.

In *The Rise of Christianity,* Rodney Stark goes even further:

> Christianity revitalized life in Greco-Roman cities by
> providing new norms and new kinds of social relation-
> ships able to cope with urgent urban problems. To cities
> filled with the homeless and impoverished, Christianity
> offered charity as well as hope. To cities filled with new-
> comers and strangers, Christianity offered an immediate
> basis for attachments. To cities filled with orphans and
> widows, Christianity provided a new and expanded sense
> of family. To cities torn by violent ethnic strife, Christian-
> ity offered a new basis for social solidarity. And to cities
> faced with epidemics, fires, and earthquakes, Christian-
> ity offered effective nursing services.[3]

Early followers of Jesus showed up and exemplified what restoration living looked like. They befriended people who were
different from them and served those in need. And somehow
along the way, evangelism took place. Stark clarifies how this
might have been possible when he concludes that most people
don't seek after a faith, but rather they "encounter one through
their ties to other people who already accept [that] faith."[4]

For the next Christians, this is predominantly how they are

seeing the church spread in the West. They show up with a restoration view, create solutions to the problems their communities face, and gently respond when spiritual conversations arise among their friends. As theologian Lesslie Newbigin observes, "Where the church is faithful to its Lord, *there* the powers of the Kingdom are present and people begin to ask the questions to which the Gospel is the answer."[5] To paraphrase the apostle Peter's admonition to the church: "Always be prepared to give a gentle and respectful answer to those who ask you about the reason for the hope [or *ought*] that is within you" (1 Pt 3:15).[6]

If this Gospel—the Gospel of Jesus Christ—is going to reengage Western culture in a new way, it starts with us. And it will happen when we commit to demonstrating his restorative power everywhere we show up and to everyone we encounter: with our friends and family, in the neighborhood where we live, and in the places where our vocations take shape. When Christians put their priority on the first thing, the second things begin to take care of themselves. Jesus himself couldn't have been any clearer: "But seek *first* his kingdom and his righteousness, and all these [second] things will be given to you as well" (Mt 6:33).

SECOND THINGS RESULTING FROM THE PROPER FIRST THINGS

I've seen many of the next Christians get the order correct. When they do, and when *we* do, consider what's possible.

The focus on savvy *outreach methods* and persuasive skills goes away. Outsiders aren't seen as commodities to be recruited, reached, or proselytized. They are treated as valued creations of God, possessing his image and seeing their goodness affirmed wherever it shines through. By recovering the Gospel, the next Christians are befriending people through authentic relationships where love is the only agenda. They trust God to work in outsiders' lives when he's ready, using their unconditional love, grace, and acceptance as the basis.

Good deeds will stop being done as an action that earns God's favor. Instead, by recovering the Gospel, Christians will recognize that ultimate grace can be experienced through Christ alone—that his unconditional love and power is the only reliable source for true restoration. Although many good deeds will go forward in his name, they will be done in a response of worship to a good God and played out in the most ordinary, and sometimes darkest, places in our world.

The emphasis placed on doing *social justice* will be grounded in the Gospel. We were once enslaved by sin, but God saved us and restored us to wholeness. So Christians plead the case of the marginalized because God pleaded their own case when *they* were marginalized.[7] Understanding this good news also means recognizing its ultimate power to change real circumstances. In the lives of the mistreated, underrepresented, and left behind of our world, the Christian responds by solving real problems. Their acts of social justice demonstrate to the world that Christ cares about the here and now—not just the afterlife.

Debates around methods of *cultural engagement* will become less of a theme. As Christians rediscover the Gospel—and particularly the life of Jesus—they will be left with only one choice: to roll their sleeves up and get in on the game. No longer content to separate or lie back hoping someone else will get involved, they are forced into the middle of society. Their sociological understanding of the seven channels of culture and the failed attempts of past generations to change culture by critiquing and condemning it inform their motivations. Instead, they show up and create culture.

For those churches trying to keep up with how to be "relevant" or debating what *church model* is most "effective," the distraction will subside. Pastors will begin to see more and more the power of the Gospel to change local communities, not just individual lives. Church leaders will disciple their people to become more like Christ, do mission in the place God has called them, and find the best way for the church structure to support those two activities.[8] The churches that recover the Gospel instead of being too focused on finding the "right" worship style, programming winsome services, or measuring church growth statistics become a light in their communities. If they left town, they'd be sorely missed. Their cities are genuinely better places, even for non-Christians, as a result of their presence.

Fascination by some Christians over *end-time prophecies* will diminish. For those who've been enamored with what life might look like around Jesus's return, they'll be awakened to their opportunity in the present moment to be a part of what God is doing now. Following the lead of the next Christians, they'll deprioritize speculation over end-time predictions by recognizing that we've all been called to restoration no matter how history's final chapter concludes.

Recovering the full story of the Gospel informs Christians on their responsibility to care for God's creation—to demonstrate *environmental stewardship*. It's not up for debate that part of our commission to "have dominion" on earth included using earth's resources responsibly, considering future generations, and doing the basic things that help creation flourish. I'm not talking about militant political action. I'm describing average Christians doing their part to limit consumption, recycle, plant gardens, and advocate for the poor where environmental injustices (like air pollution and unclean water) stand to hurt their livelihood. The Gospel of restoration extends over all of God's creation.

Church leaders will unleash their people to use their gifts throughout all seven channels of cultural influence. Understanding the Gospel's call to restore, pastors will begin to teach their people how to become vehicles for God's restoration to flood their workplaces and industries. The focus moves off *career paths* and onto calling. Christians reengage their vocations, seeing them as essential to God's original intentions for the world. The church is reignited as the focus moves from inside the walls out to every sphere of society. Along the way, people are more fulfilled as they discover purpose in the place where they are spending the majority of their time.

Finally, Christians won't be consumed with trying to *change the negative perceptions* so prevalent within the younger generations. Instead, they'll recognize that perceptions change one person at a time—one experience at a time. I once thought that Christianity's problem was "branding." But that's a second thing. The first thing is the Gospel. When Christians recover the effect of the Gospel in their own lives to shift their inclinations from judgment to grace, hypocrisy to authenticity, and rejection to acceptance, then outsiders will give them another chance. But this kind of shift won't happen instantly. The perception will only change through consistent exposure, over time, to Christ's followers who take seriously their call to proclaim and embody the Gospel in everything they do, everywhere they go.

THE CHURCH IS BREATHING NEW LIFE

The afternoon rush begins to settle as 8 p.m. arrives in Hong Kong. Over two thousand students have assembled in Queen Elizabeth Stadium for a gathering unlike anything most of them have ever experienced. Christians and the curious alike have come together, anticipating the sixteenth stop of Passion's world tour—a trip that's already hit cities across five continents on its way to the sixth, Sydney, Australia, the final destination. These students are jacked. Few Christian groups show up in China to celebrate Jesus, so this occasion has been highly anticipated. Not only are they likely to dance, raise their hands, and jump as enthusiastic worshippers in response to music designed to glorify God, but they'll also be challenged to sacrifice of themselves for those in need.

Louie and Shelley Giglio lead Passion, a college movement that's been gaining momentum for well over a decade. They focus singularly on reminding students that glorifying God with their lives is critically important. Along the way, thousands have found the answer to their individual spiritual pursuits by responding to God's invitation of grace. Many more have been called to follow Jesus in rich and vigorous ways.

Hong Kong represents just one more city, one more night, and one more venue where students will be invited to live out their Christian responsibility to restore. If it's anything like every other gathering Passion hosts, hundreds will enthusiastically respond.

In the last two years alone, students from all over the world have pooled their time, talent, and resources to build twenty-two wells in African villages; rescue at least one hundred women from Indian brothels, providing them with sustainable jobs; and build five homes where forty former Ugandan child soldiers are being restored with the help of a house mother. They've helped provide nearly three hundred children with life-altering surgeries that solve disabilities and dispatched thousands of New Testament audio translations into the hands of Sudanese refugees and Christians throughout Arab countries.[9]

A generation, written off by many as unreachable, is being galvanized by the opportunity to restore things to how they ought to be. It's truly remarkable. Most Western-educated college students aren't used to having demands placed on them to live an unselfish existence, but when someone like Louie calls, they step up. They are drawn to a faith that feels substantive and forces an alteration in their self-consumed way of life. They long for a spirituality that requires commitment and possesses a gritty, authentic quality that breaks through the superficial religious rules they've grown accustomed to ignoring.

Of course, for many of the youthful skeptics in the bunch it means they may have to experience truth before believing in it as such, but that's common among coming generations. For the next Christians, skepticism isn't to be feared, it's to be embraced. They know that for centuries God's grace has been wide enough to meet entire cultures right where they sit. They know that today's typical outsiders aren't likely to be reached through persuasive argument but instead through first experiencing an authentic Christian: someone who's willing to roll up his or her sleeves and restore alongside them.

* * *

THE THOUSANDS WHO attend Passion around the world aren't the only ones who illustrate the change happening. The church has been reignited in the West. Although few significant trend lines point to it, beyond declining church attendance statistics, an entire population of Christians is rediscovering purpose in their lives. Like new wine in new wine skins, the momentum is building in ways that elude our traditional metrics for measuring church activity. Nevertheless, a surge is under way. And though it will likely take years before it manifests itself in real, quantifiable data, connections between life, faith, and work are being made. People are coming alive and the church is sitting at the nucleus of what could be the faith's next great expansion.

No longer embarrassed to claim the label, these Christians have finally recovered what many who have gone before them always understood about the faith: namely, that the Christian view of the world informs everything, that the Gospel runs deep, and that the way of Jesus demands we give our lives in service to others. Jesus's atonement was not only meant to be a simple ticket to heaven—it carried consequence for how Christians live their lives on earth today.

A church-planting movement has swept the next Christians, and as a result, Christian communities seem to be popping up all over the place. From old abandoned warehouses and run-down bars to coffeehouses, high school auditoriums, and living room floors. The church is being replanted before our very eyes and at a rate faster than anyone can accurately calculate. Churches are scattered from chilly New England to the frothy shores of California and are not limited to any particular denomination or theological persuasion.

Pastors like Jon Tyson (Manhattan), Gideon Tsang (Austin), and Kris McDaniel (Atlanta) have moved their families into their urban centers, incarnating Christ's love at the heart of culture. Seeing every social ill as an affront to the Gospel of

Jesus, they are mobilizing entire congregations to use their gifts and talents to solve real problems in their communities. They don't just incite their people to serve: They are teaching them to think, equipping them with a full understanding of the Gospel story that they can translate when friends and neighbors raise the questions.

In the suburbs, a new generation is demanding that the church go deeper than the superficial appetites of consumer culture. They've caught a glimpse of how things ought to be and will stop at nothing to help their churches make the shift to become more restoration-minded. Some churches adopt the needs of entire neighborhoods or their local school. They are intentionally becoming aware of where their people already work and finding ways to disciple them right where they've been placed.

Bubbling just underneath the surface, the next Christians are looking for others who have found this new, old way of serving Jesus. They are on the lookout for language, stories, and models that will assist them in pioneering this new frontier. Perhaps this book will become a helpful tool.

The bottom line is that the Christian has a calling and a responsibility to think, work, and live in terms of how the world ought to be in contrast to reacting to how it really *is*. Christians who engage the world—like the many stories I've shared and the many more I could have—are consumed by this "way things ought to be" mind-set. They eat, drink, and breathe restoration. They see injustice and fight it. When confronted with evil they turn it for good. They are motivated to bring the love of Christ into every broken system they encounter. Instead of being cynical and hopeless, they bring optimism and expectation. For them, the entire world has been flipped on its head.

Their focus has moved from self *to* others; from problems *to* solutions; from failure *to* redemption; from brokenness *to* restoration. They recognize the broken, weak, fallen, and corrupt but can't leave them in that condition—they are moved to change things. The next Christians are offering a new way forward—a way to act, live, and bring others along with them into the new reality of how things *ought* to be.

This doesn't mean they are perfect. In fact, the Christians I've profiled throughout this book would all readily admit that they are in constant need of restoration themselves. Sometimes they make huge mistakes, get sidetracked, or foolishly ignore one of the six characteristics that at one point were critical in their lives. But that's what makes them so unique—they don't have it all figured out. They are messy and broken, and that doesn't stop them from engaging. From time to time, they will let us down. They will fail. I haven't shared all of their failures in this book, because that's not the point. The bigger reality is that they are just like you and me, but they haven't let their missteps stop them from pursuing God's calling in their lives and sharing his restoration power with others wherever they can.

For you, the call is literally within your grasp. It's the place you show up each day and the problems you encounter in the process. Possibly for you, it's putting a dent in the never-ending cycle of poverty that destroys so many lives, neighborhoods, and nations. Or creatively addressing the malnutrition, poor health, and disease that's wrecking so many families. Or tutoring, mentoring, and fostering fatherless children. Perhaps the addiction to drugs, alcohol, career advancement, affluence, or pornography is what enslaves and torments your friends the most. Whatever it is that's broken, whatever *you* see wrong, remember—God's intention and method of restoration is to use you to bring his redeeming love to the world.

This is the "power of the ought" at work—the way restoration living begins to flood and transform our entire cosmos. It represents Christ's power to change the world. It's playing out in the oddest of places—from overhauling the broken Texas prison system to igniting a spiritual revolution in Hong Kong. It's a way of life that's likely emerging in a neighborhood near you. And it's conceivable that God wants to use you to bring it to life.

This is the work of Jesus in the twenty-first century.

After all, didn't he announce his own mission and purpose by saying it in a similar way?

> *The Spirit of the Lord is on me,*
>   *because he has anointed me*
>   *to proclaim good news to the poor.*
> *He has sent me to proclaim freedom for the prisoners*
>   *and recovery of sight for the blind,*
> *to set the oppressed free,*
>   *to proclaim the year of the Lord's favor.*
>
> (Lk 4:18–19)

In other words, Jesus is saying, "Enough of what *is;* I see things in terms of how they *ought* to be, and I'm here to do something about it."

And from what I can tell, so are the next Christians.

We already feel the reverberations of this shift. The next Christians are breathing new life into a movement that, in some ways, was sputtering at the close of the last century. Ready for tomorrow's challenges, they turn toward the twenty-first-century horizon with grace in their hands and the Gospel as their calling. They are restoring confidence in their faith and turning "Christian" into a label worthy of the one who has called them to restore.

ACKNOWLEDGMENTS

Any important work is only made possible through the contributions of an entire community of people. I offer my personal thanks to the following:

First and foremost, I must acknowledge the work of Christ throughout my life as he has blessed me, grown me, and chiseled away the rough spots. A thousand thank-yous are insufficient for his sustaining grace.

To my family without whom this book, and life itself, would not be possible. Rebekah, my love, you are the epitome of a sacrificial, lifelong partner. You have single-handedly given me the freedom, encouragement, nourishment, and empowerment to sustain this vision. Cade, you were the inspiration that first sent us on this journey and continue to foster my view of God. Pierce, thank you for listening to Daddy read excerpts. Even at the age of six, you make me feel like a literary giant. Kennedy, you are a doll and a natural leader . . . and, yes, now this book is "finally in the store!" Children, I pray you are inspired and challenged every day to become the kind of Jesus follower I describe in this book.

To the mentors in my life, I offer special thanks. You have not only profoundly shaped this book but the person who wrote it. Chuck Colson and Louie Giglio, your clarity of calling and specificity of message to an entire generation guides my own.

Michael Metzger, Os Guinness, and Tim Keller, patient teachers and visionary leaders, thank you for giving me a lens through which to see the Gospel more clearly.

To my closest friends, who shape my thinking and keep me humble. I especially thank Jason Locy. Your honesty and commitment over the last seven years is without price. Brad Lomenick, Ken Coleman, and Tim Willard, your input has been critical and our "guys nights" a priceless respite as we processed together what this means for our lives.

To my unofficial editorial team. Norton Herbst, your help charting out this book gave me the confidence to write it. Ben Ortlip, your vision and masterful coaching to ensure my voice came through has made me—an otherwise pretty boring person—seem interesting! Andy Stanley, Bob Buford, Brent Cole, Corey Mazer, John Adams, Nancy Becker, and Shannon Mescher—thank you for carefully reading my earliest drafts and offering critical feedback. The fruits of your efforts mark each page. Finally, Jonathan Merritt, your tireless efforts to make my writing stronger and waste zero words are lessons I take with me into future projects. You helped me bring it across the line.

To my agent, Chris Ferebee, thank you for providing wisdom, friendship, and representation. To the entire Doubleday team led by Michael Palgon and Trace Murphy, thank you for the profound investment of hard work and critical thinking.

To all the others who have played a significant role in my life but whose names did not appear due to the limited space, I extend my personal thanks. You know who you are.

NOTES

ONE | A FADING REALITY

1. American Religious Identification Survey statistics: Barry A. Kosmin and Ariela Keysar, ARIS 2008 (Hartford, Connecticut: Trinity College, 2008), 3.

2. If you don't believe me, ask these questions: When was the last time a leader of your church participated in a city council meeting? When did your church last host a civic event unrelated to church programming? How recently has your city government or school system sought out and consulted your church for wisdom or assistance regarding a need? Sure enough, this is happening in some places in wonderful ways, but it's more the exception than the rule.

TWO | THE NEW NORMAL

1. Sue Lindsey, "Rev. Jerry Falwell, Founder of Moral Majority, Dies at 73," Associated Press, May 16, 2007; http://www.nctimes.com/news/local/article_defe8407-1d63-5212-9a5e-760de7bd18f2.html.

2. Christopher Hitchens, interview by Anderson Cooper, *Anderson Cooper 360°*, CNN, May 15, 2007; http://transcripts.cnn.com/TRANSCRIPTS/0705/15/acd.01.html (accessed May 22, 2009).

3. Jon Meacham, "The End of Christian America," *Newsweek*, April 13, 2009; http://www.newsweek.com/id/192583.

4. *Zeitgeist: The Movie*, directed by Joseph Smith, 2007; http://www.zeitgeistmovie.com/transcript.htm (accessed May 26, 2009).

5. Ibid.

6. The public square doesn't refer to a physical location like the town courthouse, American Congress, or British Parliament. Rather, it is a metaphor for all the forums in which citizens can come together to deliberate, debate, and decide the implications of their common life. See Os Guinness, *The Case for Civility* (San Francisco: HarperOne, 2008), 14.

7. Diana Eck, *A New Religious America: The World's Most Religiously Diverse Nation* (San Francisco: HarperOne, 2002), 432.

8. Robert Wuthnow, *After the Baby Boomers: How Twenty- and Thirty-Somethings Are Shaping the Future of American Religion* (Princeton, N.J.: Princeton University Press, 2007), 48.

9. It should be noted that a pluralistic public square was the intention of the founding fathers. The founding of America was certainly influenced by Christian values, but contrary to what some may think, most historians agree that the nation was not established to be a sacred "Christian nation."

10. Doug Huntington, "Hindu to Lead Prayer in U.S. Senate for First Time Ever," *Christian Post,* July 3, 2007; http://www.christianpost.com/article/20070703/hindu-to-lead-prayer-in-u-s-senate-for-first-time-ever/index.html.

11. Os Guinness, *The Case for Civility*, 22.

12. "Faith in Flux: Changes in Religious Affiliation in the U.S." Pew Forum on Religion and Public Life, April 27, 2009; http://pewforum.org/PublicationPage.aspx?id=1154.

13. Robert Wuthnow, *After the Baby Boomers*, 52.

14. Rogier Bos, "Next-Wave Interview with Stanley J. Grenz," *Next Wave,* May 1999; http://www.next-wave.org/may99/sg.htm.

15. Modernity is the era in the Western world that took place from the late 1500s to the mid-1900s. It was defined by the conviction that the world was organized through a set of abstract principles—the laws of logic, physics, mathematics, and economics—and that humans only had to work to discover these laws, classify and systematize them, and ultimately leverage them for the sake of progress and betterment of society. "Enlightenment" was within humanity's grasp. Through rational thought, scientific experimentation, and dogged determination, humans could achieve

anything they wanted. It was only a matter of time before humanity's utopian ideals would be reached. Postmodernity—the era that now governs the West—deconstructs all of that. In postmodernity, the promises of modernism are exposed as hollow. Authority is questioned, individuals are autonomous, and truth is relative.

16. The "West" refers to cultures with a "European" foundation: Western Europe, the United Kingdom, Australia, New Zealand, Canada, and the United States.

17. *Q Society Room: Where You Live Matters,* DVD (Grand Rapids, MI: Zondervan, 2010). See Joel Kotkin's Q Talk called "The Future of the Suburbs," http://www.qideas.org.

18. Rob Bell, interview by Gabe Lyons, *Catalyst Podcast,* episode 6 (June 23, 2006).

19. See Alan Hirsch and Michael Frost, *The Shaping of Things to Come* (Kitchener, ON: Henrickson, 2003), for the language of "periphery."

20. "Spirituality in America," *Newsweek,* August 21, 2005; http://www.newscom.com/cgi-bin/prnh/20050821/NYSU005 (accessed November 23, 2009).

21. Jerry Adler, "In Search of the Spiritual," *Newsweek,* August 29, 2005; http://www.newsweek.com/id/147035/page/1 (accessed November 23, 2009).

22. *Newsweek*'s official survey found 45 percent; the U.S. Pew Forum recently found that number to be 39 percent. *Newsweek* journalists suggest that "there is probably a fair amount of wishful thinking in those figures; researchers who have done actual head counts in churches think the figure is probably more like 20 percent."

23. See http://www.prnewswire.com/cgi-bin/stories.pl?ACCT=104& STORY=/www/story/08-21-2005/0004091628&EDATE (accessed November 23, 2009).

THREE | A PARODY OF OURSELVES

1. *Glassroth v. Moore,* U.S. District Court, Middle District of Alabama, 4; http://fl1.findlaw.com/news.findlaw.com/hdocs/docs/religion/glsrthmre111802opn.pdf (accessed May 29, 2009).

2. This quote was taken from a Fox News story that aired on August 27, 2003.

3. Cultural warriors believe that the founding fathers' intent was to set up and maintain America as a "Sacred Christian Nation," meaning that our nation was designed for Christian beliefs to remain at the center of its society—even at the exclusion and silencing of others. This view motivates Christians like the Roy's Rock angry supporter to ensure that societal values and cultural artifacts reflect our founders' historic belief in Christianity, even when society no longer behaves, thinks, or seeks the Christian God. This view is so prominent in America today that 66 percent of evangelical Christians believe it would be good to pass an amendment to the Constitution making Christianity the official religion of the United States. See the Barna Research Group statistics at http://www.barna.org/barna-update/article/5-barnaupdate/192-how-qchristianizedq-do-americans-want-their-country-to-be (accessed May 29, 2009).

    It undergirds much of the motivation that has driven the Religious Right movement for decades and is responsible for much of the acrimony in the "Christian v. Secular" war today.

    Many good Christians may try to disagree, but a deeper look at our history, the Constitution, and the framers themselves reveals that America was not created to be a "Sacred Christian Nation." Rather our founding fathers constructed a Constitution and created a nation where different religions could be safely practiced. They removed religious disenfranchisement (the very reason many of their own ancestors had left England) from the equation. As Os Guinness points out, "The religious-liberty clauses are a wise provision for ordering religion and public life, simultaneously addressing the demands of freedom, justice, and order, and allowing us to live with our deepest differences, so that diversity remains a source of strength rather than weakness." See Guinness, *The Case for Civility,* 47.

4. Ezekiel 3:18–19 is often taken out of context: "When I say to the wicked, 'You shall surely die,' and you give him no warning, nor speak to warn the wicked from his wicked way, to save his life,

that same wicked man shall die in his iniquity; but his blood I will require at your hand. Yet, if you warn the wicked, and he does not turn from his wickedness, nor from his wicked way, he shall die in his iniquity; but you have delivered your soul."

5. I'm not suggesting that evangelism isn't central to the Christian faith. The point is that this group has come to believe that evangelism is the *only* thing that defines the Christian faith.

6. Alister McGrath, *Christianity's Dangerous Idea: The Protestant Revolution—A History from the Sixteenth Century to the Twenty-First* (San Francisco: HarperOne, 2007), 392.

7. Ibid.

8. David Kinnaman and Gabe Lyons, *UnChristian: What a New Generation Really Thinks About Christianity . . . And Why It Matters* (Grand Rapids, MI: Baker, 2007), 48.

9. This is a bit ironic since many churches that are pursuing "relevance" above everything else are driven by an "evangelizer's" mentality.

10. See James 2:14–26.

11. Whatever the motive, churches that produce Cultural Christians often thrive on service and compassion ministries—so much so that Separatist Christians label them "liberal" and accuse them of "watering down the Gospel." Much of this goes back to a movement of Christians in the late nineteenth and early twentieth centuries that promoted a "Social Gospel," that is, a message that places greater emphasis on overturning social injustice than stressing doctrine or evangelism. And as you might guess, the Fundamentalists denounced these liberal Christians. The tension between these two understandings of how Christians should live out their faith remains today.

12. The word "Pharisee" actually meant "Separatist" in Greek.

13. See Scot McKnight, *The Jesus Creed: Loving God, Loving Others* (Brewster, MA: Paraclete Press, 2004), 36.

14. Craig L. Blomberg, *Contagious Holiness: Jesus' Meals with Sinners* (Downers Grove, IL: InterVarsity Press, 2005), 167.

15. Ibid.

FOUR | RELEARNING RESTORATION

1. Tom Wolfe, "The Great Relearning," *American Spectator,* December 1987, 14.

2. In other words, this view of the Gospel message reduces the Bible's grand story down to two primary "chapters": Fall and Redemption. Indeed, these two chapters are central to the biblical narrative, but historic Christian orthodoxy has always held that there is a foundational chapter to the story before the Fall and a climactic chapter in the story after Redemption.

3. See the introductory chapters of N. T. Wright, *Simply Christian: Why Christianity Makes Sense* (San Francisco: HarperOne, 2006).

4. Metzger, Michael, *Our Terms for Cultural Influence* (Annapolis: The Clapham Institute, 2002), 19.

5. Biblical scholar Scot McKnight has noted that when humanity fell into sin, four primary relationships were broken: our relationships with God, ourselves, others, and creation. God's intentions are that we would experience restoration in all four of these relationships, a goal that ultimately finds its fulfillment when he makes all things new (Rev 21:5).

6. Todd Tucker, *The Great Starvation Experiment: The Heroic Men Who Starved So That Millions Could Live* (New York: Free Press, 2006).

7. I first heard this idea explained by Michael Metzger. He describes the four-part telling of the Gospel story in terms more common to those outside the Christian faith with less pretense than our typical terms. He uses common language like "ought, is, can, will" to delineate the four-part Gospel.

8. Quoted from "The PEP Story," http://pep.org/who/story.aspx (accessed May 26, 2009).

9. Since my inclusion of Catherine Rohr's story in the initial manuscript, she resigned from her role as president and CEO of the Prison Entrepreneurship Program following six years of service. Her resignation came after her self-admission of "inappropriately close relationships with four free men who were also PEP graduates." She states in her resignation letter that these poor decisions came as a result of a "costly departure from my spiritual

values" and a withdrawal "from my community of support and accountability."

Both of these statements only further highlight the importance of staying grounded and in community (chapters 8 and 9). I chose to keep Catherine's story in the final manuscript because despite her leadership failure, her "ought" view of the world perfectly captures the difference it can exponentially make in others' lives as it continues to surge forward in Texas prisons. Also by including it, I hope to practice what this book preaches—which is to celebrate the moments we allow God to carry out his restoration work through us, even though we are flawed human beings. http://files.e2ma.net/16250/assets/docs/catherine_rohr__s_resignation_announcement.pdf.

10. T. S. Eliot, *Christianity and Culture* (Fort Washington, PA: Harvest Books, 1960), 6.

FIVE | PROVOKED, *NOT OFFENDED*

1. See http://www.twloha.com/vision/story/ for the full story on To Write Love on Her Arms.
2. Michael Metzger wrote an extensive piece on this called "Navigating Tensions" that we read for an original Q Society Room meeting I put together. This piece has never been published but it takes a deeper look at the kind of conscience that is necessary in order to explore proximity while maintaining purity. He describes this concept at a much deeper level than this chapter will address. His latest book, *Sequencing: Deciphering Your Company's DNA*, explores this concept further.
3. Eugene Peterson, *The Jesus Way: A Conversation on the Ways That Jesus Is the Way* (Grand Rapids, MI: Eerdmans, 2007), 211.
4. It should also be noted that Jesus even engaged the Pharisees themselves—the ones whose hearts he knew were so cold and misguided (Lk 7, 11, 14; Jn 3).
5. Luke 19:10 (MSG; emphasis added).
6. Not because judgment of non-Christians is never deserved, but because this is the Holy Spirit's role (Jn 16:8–11), not ours.

7. John Stott talks more about the city of Athens in his book *Christian Mission in the Modern World: What the Church Should Be Doing Now!* (Downers Grove, IL: InterVarsity Press, 1974).

8. E. M. Blaiklock, *The Acts of the Apostles: An Historical Commentary* (Grand Rapids, MI: Eerdmans, 1959).

SIX | CREATORS, *NOT CRITICS*

1. Josh Jackson and Nick Purdy, interview by Will Hinton, GoodWill Hinton.com, May 26, 2009; http://goodwillhinton.com/good_will_hinton_interviews_paste_magazine.

2. Named "Best Magazine of the Year" by the PLUG Independent Music Awards, 2006, 2007, 2008. Received 2007 and 2008 National Magazine Award General Excellence nominations.

3. Stott, *Christian Mission in the Modern World,* 27.

4. Michael S. Sherwin, *St. Thomas and the Common Good* (Rome: Pontificia Universita San Tommaso, 1993), 315. Susanne M. DeCrane cites Sherwin's work about St. Thomas's view in *Aquinas, Feminism, and the Common Good* (Washington, D.C.: Georgetown University Press, 2004): "A community which prevents even one of its citizens from attaining this ultimate good in any way he or she has been divinely called is not ordering the community's good or the divine good" (73).

5. Andy Crouch, *Culture Making* (Downers Grove, IL: InterVarsity Press, 2008), 67.

6. I first heard this phrase from Nick Purdy and Josh Jackson, founders of *Paste* magazine. Andy Crouch also uses this terminology to describe culture.

7. Jason Locy and Tim Willard, "Veneer: A Commentary on Culture and the Church," Q Essay (2008), http://www.qideas.org.

8. Pierre Ruhe, "Fringe Atlanta's Most Excellent Debut," *Atlanta Journal Constitution,* September 23, 2007.

9. Wright, *Simply Christian,* 44.

10. Dr. Clifford Hill, in *Creating the Better Hour: Lessons from William Wilberforce,* ed. Chuck Stetson (Macon, GA: Stroud and Hall, 2004), 94.

11. Jeremy Cowart and Jena Lee, *Hope in the Dark* (Relevant Books, 2006).

12. Klaus Bockmuehl, *The Christian Way of Living: An Ethics of the Ten Commandments* (Vancouver, B.C.: Regent College Publishing, 1997), 25–26.

13. Tim Keller, "A New Kind of Urban Christian," *Christianity Today* 50 (May 2006): 36.

14. Amy Harmon, "Prenatal Test Puts Down Syndrome in Hard Focus," *New York Times,* May 9, 2007; http://www.nytimes.com/2007/05/09/us/09down.html. For further reading, see Caroline Mansfield, Suellen Hopfer, and Theresa M. Marteau, "Termination Rates After Prenatal Diagnosis of Down Syndrome, Spina Bifida, Anencephaly, and Turner and Klinefelter Syndromes: A Systematic Literature Review," *Prenatal Diagnosis* 19 (9): 808–12.

15. Ibid.

16. Andrew Pollack, "Blood Tests Ease Search for Down Syndrome," *New York Times,* October 6, 2008; http://www.nytimes.com/2008/10/07/health/research/07down.html.

SEVEN | CALLED, *NOT EMPLOYED*

1. David Brooks, "People Like Us," *Atlantic Monthly,* September 2003; http://www.theatlantic.com/doc/200309/brooks.

2. Bob Briner used the term "second-class Christians" in his seminal work, *Roaring Lambs* (Grand Rapids, MI: Zondervan, 1993).

3. Paul Rondeau, "Selling Homosexuality to America Essay," *Regent University Law Review* 14, no. 2 (2001–2002): 445.

4. Ibid.

5. *Corporate Equality Index* (Human Rights Campaign, 2006); www.hrc.org.

6. Steve Inskeep, "Openly Gay Bishop Consecrated by Episcopal Church," interview by Barbara Bradley Hagerty, *All Things Considered,* National Public Radio, November 2, 2003.

7. Charles Colson and Nancy Pearcey, *How Now Shall We Live?* (Carol Streams, IL: Tyndale House Publishers, 1999), 33.

8. Ibid.

9.   Rick Warren, *The Purpose Driven Life: What on Earth Am I Here For?* (Grand Rapids, MI: Zondervan, 2002).

10.   Learn more at http://www.charitywater.org.

11.   These words are traditionally attributed to Goethe's *Faust,* a play completed in 1832 and loosely translated into English in 1835. However, recent research has demonstrated that the first portion of these lines originated with W. H. Murray in his 1951 book *The Scottish Himalayan Expedition.*

EIGHT | GROUNDED, NOT DISTRACTED

1.   Douglas Connelly, *Daniel: Spiritual Living in a Secular World* (Downers Grove, IL: InterVarsity Press, 2000), 10.

2.   Andy Crouch, "From Purchases to Practices," Q Essay (2008), 12. For more information about Q Essays, go to http://www.qideas.org.

3.   See 2008 U.S. Bureau of Labor statistics at http://www.bls.gov/news.release/atus.t01.htm (accessed November 23, 2009).

4.   The cultural observer David Henderson highlights entertainment's impact:

> The trouble is that the channels of entertainment—and television [being] the chief culprit—disorient more than they orient. Promising to make sense of the world for us, they merely multiply the collage of disconnected images and sounds and experiences that come at us.

As Neil Postman famously wrote, we are "amusing ourselves to death."

Perhaps the seventeenth-century philosopher Pascal explains our obsession with entertainment and its consequences well when he writes, "Diversion prevents us from thinking about ourselves." Maybe entertainment just distracts us from acknowledging our truly broken condition. And this distraction is dangerous and real. Pascal wisely points out that without diversion (or, for our discussion, *entertainment*), "we should be bored, and boredom would drive us to seek some more solid means of escape, but diversion passes our time and brings us imperceptibly to our death." Neil Postman's book *Amusing Ourselves to Death* was published in 1985 and conveyed many of the important conceptions of Marshall MacLuhan's writings from the 1960s related to how technology shapes humanity.

For further reading see Blaise Pascal, *Pensées,* ed. Alban Krailsheimer (New York: Penguin, 1966), 414, 171, and David W. Henderson, *Culture Shift: Communicating God's Truth to Our Changing World* (Grand Rapids, MI: Baker Books, 1998), 71.

5. This one change alone alters how many perceive and interact with Scripture. Instead of a reference book (chapter and verse numbers), it becomes a moving novel or screenplay.

6. Rob Bell and I had a discussion about the Sabbath during which he made this statement. It's taken from my interview with him on the *Catalyst Podcast,* episode 6 (June 23, 2006).

7. Later, when God gave Israel the law, keeping the Sabbath— resting from our work on the seventh day of the week—was listed as one of the Ten Commandments (Ex 20:8–11). What's more, the Sabbath wasn't limited to just resting from work one day a week; it also encompassed taking time to celebrate religious holidays (Lv 16:31) and giving the land a rest from agricultural production each seventh year (Lv 25:2–7).

8. J. C. McCann Jr., "Sabbath," in *The International Standard Bible Encyclopedia,* 4th ed., ed. Geoffrey W. Bromiley (Grand Rapids, MI: Eerdmans, 1988), 247–52.

9. *Shmita* is the agricultural cycle that is mandated in the Torah. For more information on the science of shmita, see http://jewish publicaffairs.blog.com/Shmita/ (accessed May 28, 2009).

10. The Jewish writer Abraham Joshua Heschel says that the Sabbath "gives the world the energy it needs to live for another six days." For further reading on the Sabbath, I would suggest Heschel's *The Sabbath* (New York: Farrar Straus Giroux, 2005).

11. Bell, *Catalyst Podcast,* episode 6.

12. As Mark Buchanan puts it, the discipline of practicing the Sabbath is an invitation to *stop.* It is a way to take a day off every week from the typical habits and artificial appetites of our world.

13. See Scot McKnight, *Fasting: The Ancient Practices* (Nashville: Thomas Nelson, 2009) for one of the best treatments of the subject.

14. Dallas Willard, *The Divine Conspiracy: Recovering Our Hidden Life in God* (San Francisco: HarperOne, 1998), 166. Don Colbert, M.D., says that fasting has great physical benefits as well. "Fasting does not only prevent sickness. If done correctly, fasting holds amazing healing benefits to those of us who suffer illness and disease. From colds and flus to heart disease, fasting is a mighty key to healing the body." See his book *Toxic Relief* (Lake Mary, FL: Siloam, 2003), 155.

15. But the pursuit of having "more" is paradoxical because it actually gives you "less." Henry David Thoreau famously experienced this when he set out to escape the developing world and spend two years alone on Walden Pond in a cabin he built by hand. In *Walden,* his 1854 essay, he observes that "most of the luxuries, and many of the so-called comforts, of life are not only not indispensable, but positive hindrances to the elevation of mankind." He understood that the more we consume, the less we become human. We become bound by our obsession for physical things and end up living within the rut of an overextended lifestyle, all to the beat of the American dream's drum.

16. Giles Slade, *Made to Break: Technology and Obsolescence in America* (Cambridge, MA: Harvard University Press, 2006), 6–7.

17. See Facebook statistics at http://www.facebook.com/press/info .php?statistics (accessed May 28, 2009).

18. The Styrofoam robot is an artistic creation he and his daughter cobbled together from three years of discarded shipping foam.

NINE | IN COMMUNITY, *NOT ALONE*

1. Robert Putnam, *Bowling Alone: The Collapse and Revival of American Community* (New York: Simon & Schuster, 2001), 403. Putnam draws the contrast perfectly when he notes in his book that during the first two-thirds of the twentieth century, Americans engaged in social and political life, gave to charity, pitched in on

community projects, and usually trusted one another. But something significant changed in the last third of the century. Community involvement dramatically declined, and reliance on a steady collective of friends evaporated, even though both were once viewed as critical for sanity, grounding, and a full life.

2. Ibid., 284. The pie chart (figure 79) shows how the decline in civic involvement has manifested.

3. See Seth Godin's *Tribes: We Need You to Lead Us* (New York: Portfolio Hardcover, 2008).

4. For example, see 1 Corinthians 12.

5. Michael Metzger, "The Story of Community," unpublished essay, the Clapham Group, 11.

6. Ibid.

7. Hill, *Creating the Better Hour,* 20.

8. Viscountess Knutsford, as cited ibid.

9. Metzger, "The Story of Community," 11.

10. Rodney Stark, *The Rise of Christianity* (San Francisco: HarperOne, 1997), 55.

11. Ibid., 82.

12. Wright, *Simply Christian,* 123.

13. Ibid.

14. When Moses received the Ten Commandments and law from God, consider how he passed them on to the entire nation:

> See, I [Moses] have taught you [Israel] decrees and laws as the LORD my God commanded me, so that you may follow them in the land you are entering to take possession of it. Observe them carefully, for this will show your wisdom and understanding to the nations, who will hear about all these decrees and say, "Surely this great nation is a wise and understanding people." What other nation is so great as to have their gods near them the way the LORD our God is near us whenever we pray to him? And what other nation is so great as to have such righteous decrees and laws as this body of laws I am setting before you today?

(Dt 4:5–8)

When the Israelites worshipped God, consider the songs they sang and why:

> *Sing to the LORD a new song;*
>   *sing to the LORD, all the earth.*
> *Sing to the LORD, praise his name;*
>   *proclaim his salvation day after day.*
> *Declare his glory among the nations,*
>   *his marvelous deeds among all peoples.*
>
>   (Ps 96:1–3)

When Solomon built the grand temple where the Hebrew people would offer sacrifices, pray, and repent before God, consider his prayer for those outside the community:

> As for the foreigners who do not belong to your people Israel but have come from a distant land because of your name—for they will hear of your great name and your mighty hand and your outstretched arm—when they come and pray toward this temple, then hear from heaven, your dwelling place. Do whatever the foreigners ask of you, so that all the peoples of the earth may know your name and fear you, as do your own people Israel, and may know that this house I have built bears your Name.   (1 Kgs 8:41–43)

Ultimately, Israel rebelled against God and rarely succeeded in accomplishing this wider mission to the nations around them, but it would be wrong to believe this was God's intent—that Israel only served God's plan as a launching point for him to send a Messiah into the world. Rather, Israel, as a community of people embodying God's restoration promise, *was* God's plan. And it found its ultimate fulfillment when Jesus *became* Israel, accepting her judgment upon himself, embracing her mission, and re-creating a new community of people that through his power would bring salvation and restoration to all the peoples of the earth. We are now part of that community.

15. Throughout the Old Testament, God called people who believed in him and followed him to be in community. In fact, for the Hebrew people, their nation was to be a community of faith: a place where they could learn from one another, encourage each other, and be on a mission together to embody God's values for the world. See Mark Lau Branson, "Forming God's People," *Congregations* 29 (Winter 2003): 22–27.

TEN | COUNTERCULTURAL, NOT "RELEVANT"

1. *Encarta: Dictionary,* s.v. "relevant"; http://encarta.msn.com/ dictionary (accessed May 28, 2009).
2. Bob Buford, author of *Halftime* and founder of Leadership, shared with me this direct quote from Peter Drucker, who made this statement to him in a personal conversation.
3. Colson and Pearcey, *How Now Shall We Live?* 33.
4. Eugene Peterson, *The Jesus Way* (Grand Rapids, MI: Eerdmans, 2007), 18.
5. Shane Claiborne, "What If Jesus Meant All That Stuff?" *Esquire,* November 18, 2009; http://www.esquire.com/features/best-and-brightest-2009/shane-claiborne-1209.
6. John Foyston, "Church Leaders, Mayor Sam Adams Turn Out for Season of Service Launch," *The Oregonian,* February 26, 2009; http://www.oregonlive.com/living/index.ssf/2009/02/ church_leaders_mayor_sam_adams.html (accessed April 13, 2010).
7. Tom Krattenmaker, "Evangelism 2.0," *USA Today,* July 20, 2009; http://blogs.usatoday.com/oped/2009/07/evangelism-20-.html (accessed April 13, 2010).
8. Aaron Mesh, "Undercover Jesus," *Willamette Week Online,* May 20, 2009; http://wweek.com/editorial/3528/12567/ (accessed April 13, 2010).
9. Keller, "A New Kind of Urban Christian," 56.
10. See Luke 10:29–37.
11. Cornelius Plantinga Jr., *Not the Way It's Supposed to Be: A Breviary of Sin* (Grand Rapids, MI: Eerdmans, 1995), 8.

12. Stanley Hauerwas and William H. Willimon, *Resident Aliens: Life in the Christian Colony* (Nashville: Abingdon Press, 1989), 94.

13. Cyril Richardson, ed., *Early Christian Fathers* (New York: Simon & Schuster, 1996), 175. Note: From the primary document "The So-Called Letter to Diognetus: The Mystery of the New People."

ELEVEN | THE NEXT BIG SHIFT

1. Phyllis Tickle, *The Great Emergence: How Christianity Is Changing and Why* (Grand Rapids, MI: Baker Books, 2001).

2. C. S. Lewis, *First and Second Things* (Fount, 1985), 22.

3. Rodney Stark, *The Rise of Christianity* (San Franciso: HarperOne, 1997), 161.

4. Ibid., 56.

5. Lesslie Newbigin, *The Gospel in a Pluralistic Society* (Grand Rapids, MI: Eerdmans, 1989), 119.

6. 1 Peter 3:15 says, "But in your hearts revere Christ as Lord. Always be prepared to give an answer to everyone who asks you to give the reason for the hope that you have. But do this with gentleness and respect."

7. One of the most repeated commands in the Old Testament takes this form: "Do not oppress a foreigner; you yourselves know how it feels to be foreigners, because you were foreigners in Egypt" (Ex 23:9; see also Lv 19:33–34; Ex 22:21; Dt 10:19; 23:7).

8. This idea comes out of Alan Hirsch and Michael Frost's reflections about living in a post-Christendom setting. Alan remarked during a Q Podcast interview that "Christology determines Missiology which affects Ecclesiology." See http://www.qideas.org for more on this idea.

9. See http://www.onemillioncan.com.

INDEX

IDEAS THAT CREATE A BETTER WORLD

Continue your learning and understanding of
how to express your faith in a post-Christian culture.

WATCH Q TALKS
READ Q ESSAYS
START A Q SOCIETY ROOM

Find out more at www.Qideas.org

Q
NOTES

*Continue your learning around
the topics explored in this book at*
www.nextchristians.com/Q

CHAPTER 1

A Fading Reality

- What are the challenges faced by the church in the 21st Century? See Os Guinness's talk, "Third Mission to the West."

CHAPTER 4

Relearning Restoration

- Did Jesus preach the Gospel and how was his "good news" different from what many Christians preach today? Watch New Testament scholar, Scot McKnight, as he asks "Did Jesus Preach the Gospel?"

- Have we come to believe in a Gospel that is limited? Read Tim Keel's essay, "Reframing the Gospel."

CHAPTER 5

Provoked, Not Offended

- What is the difference between being provoked and offended and how should the Gospel shape our response to culture? Read Micheal Metzger's thoughts in "Living the Gospel in Culture."

- How are followers of Jesus called to respond to sin and corruption? Watch minister and author Jo Saxton's talk, "Being Provoked to Engage."

CHAPTER 8

Grounded, Not Distracted

- How do we begin recovering spiritual disciplines in everyday life? See Phyllis Tickle's talk on "Recovering the Ancient Practices."

- How important is pausing regularly to stop consuming, refrain from working, and spend more time with our families and in worship? Watch environmentalist and author Matthew Sleeth's talk, "Observing the Sabbath."

CHAPTER 9

In Community, Not Alone

- How important are sacred spaces to fostering genuine community? Hear an interview with Mel McGowan on "A Theology of Place."

- What does it mean to be in a community known by its love? View author and pastor Leroy Barber's talk, "Beloved Community."

CHAPTER 2

The New Normal

- Could it be possible that the Judeo-Christian America we've become accustomed to is gone forever? See historian and biographer David Aikman's talk, "The End of Christian America."

CHAPTER 3

A Parody of Ourselves

- What does a new generation think about Christians and how can we begin changing that perception? Read David Kinnaman and Gabe Lyons's essay, "Unchristian: Change the Perception."

- How should we posture ourselves with regard to a fallen culture as followers of Jesus? Social activist and author Antonio Carlos Costa discusses the wide range of possibilities in his talk, "Social Activism."

CHAPTER 6

Creators, Not Critics

- How can creating something new promote the good, true, and beautiful in culture? See *Paste* magazine founders Josh Jackson and Nick Purdy's talk "Signs of Life."

- Want to see a picture of creating something beautiful in response to brokenness? Watch Jamie Tworkowski tell the story of how "To Write Love on Her Arms" began.

CHAPTER 7

Called, Not Employed

- How does what we do with our lives shape culture? Watch author Andy Crouch's talk "Stepping into Culture."

- What can we learn about calling from an MTV producer? See Owen Leimbach's talk, "Think MTV."

CHAPTER 10

Countercultural, Not "Relevant"

- Could it be that our concept and pursuit of "relevance" is grossly mistaken? Read author Chris Haw's essay, "The Relevance of Our Irrelevance."

- What would it look like to be a counterculture for the common good? Watch Jon Tyson's talk on "Advancing the Common Good."

CHAPTER 11

The Next Big Shift

- How can we begin living life in light of the way things were intended to be? See Ambassador Max Kampelman's talk, "The Power of the Ought."

- How should the church adapt and live in this new world? See missiologist Alan Hirsch's talk, "Post-Christendom Mission."

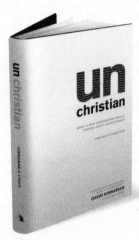